Life Preservers

Life Preservers

Staying Afloat in Love and Life

Harriet Lerner, Ph.D.

HarperPerennial

A Division of HarperCollinsPublishers

HarperCollins books may be purchased for educational, business, or sales promotional use. For information please write: International Sales Department, HarperCollins Publishers, Inc., 10 East 53rd Street, New York, NY 10022.

FIRST INTERNATIONAL EDITION

Designed by Nancy Singer

ISBN 0-06-092777-1

96 97 98 99 00 ❖/RRD 10 9 8 7 6 5 4 3 2 1

To my mother, Rose Goldhor,
life preserver, anchor, and friend

Acknowledgments

*L*ife Preservers happened this way: In 1989 Stephanie von Hirschberg invited me to write a monthly advice column for *New Woman* magazine. My husband, Steve, no slouch with good advice himself, encouraged me to say yes to her offer and later suggested that I write this book. My friend Carol Tavris came up with the title, thus sparing the world yet another *Dance* book. I am very grateful.

Many others have helped along the way. My dear friends Jeffrey Ann Goudie and Tom Averill have been improving my manuscripts and encouraging my work for so many years that it's difficult to find fresh ways to thank them. I can't imagine the writing life without their encouragement and abundant editorial support. Peternelle van Arsdale at HarperCollins inherited this project in its final stages and proved to be amazingly "on target" as an editor, capable of working at warp speed. And HarperCollins, my publisher of over a decade, has remained committed to my work.

Stephanie von Hirschberg, senior editor at *New*

Woman magazine, deserves special thanks for her particular combination of wisdom, integrity, and heart. And Betsy Carter, editor-in-chief of *New Woman,* continues to provide enthusiastic support for "Harriet Lerner's Good Advice," as do the magazine's many appreciative readers.

At The Menninger Clinic, my home base, Mary Ann Clifft improves everything I write with her sharp editorial eye and meticulous attention to detail. Ellen Safier, my friend and colleague a few doors down, keeps startling me with her generous and bountiful creativity. Emily Kofron, Jeffrey Ann Goudie, Judie Koontz, Nancy Maxwell, and Marianne Ault-Riché have been my intimate friends and loyal readers for many years and are always there for me, no matter what. And my husband, Steve, and our two sons, Matt and Ben, ground me in the world and remind me how lucky I am to have my family.

Special thanks to Katherine Kent, who has generously shared her expertise on family and work systems over many years and whose ideas and words I draw upon often. I'm also grateful for the pioneering work of the late Murray Bowen, the founder of natural systems theory, and for the inspiring presence of consultant and teacher Carolyn Conger. Thanks also to my friend and good neighbor Janet Paisley, and to Vonda Lohness-Sieh, Marjorie Shoemaker, Lisa Liebman, Georgia Kolias, Chuck Baird, Nanette Gartrell, Diana Laskin Siegal, Meredith Titus, Karen Schuss Rowinksy, Libby Rosen, Eleanor Bell, Susan Liening, Mark Levine, Susan Kraus, Mark Sommer, Jen Hofer, Brenda Woodward, Kristen Auclair, Suzanne Noli, Lisa Desimini, Penni Gladstone, and especially to Joanie Shoemaker, for their assorted contributions to *Life Preservers.*

I want to thank Janet Goldstein and Bill Shinker, who gave me my start in publishing and whose vision and insight launched and nurtured my career as a writer. And finally, I owe the greatest debt to Jo-Lynne Worley, my manager and friend, who has worked second hardest on this book and who is an invisible collaborator in all my projects. I thank her for her remarkable competence, her unwavering good judgment, her unflappable patience and generosity, and for standing by me and believing in me since we teamed up in the fall of 1990.

I feel more than lucky to be surrounded by so many amazing souls who have demonstrated the tenacity of love and friendship by sticking with me through so many years, so many manuscripts, and who will, I hope, be with me through many more.

Contents

2 Mending the Mind, Body, and Spirit

3 Friendship Matters

4 Women at Work

5   No Place Like Home

6   Then Comes Marriage

7 Parents in Recovery

8 The World We Love In

To My Readers

There are never just two different ways to understand or tackle any particular human problem. There are seven different ways—or maybe nineteen or one hundred. Sometimes imagination and *un*common sense are required to solve the riddles and relationships of life.

I'm a person who asks for help. I don't always apply my best thinking to my own problems (compared to, say, someone *else's* problems). If I'm anxious enough, or angry enough, I may not think at all. That's when I grab some remarkably clear-thinking person by the collar and ask what *she* thinks or what *he* would do in my shoes. At a calmer time, I may be the remarkably clear-thinking person someone else needs.

Some folks are "do-it-yourselfers," but emotional self-sufficiency doesn't appeal to me. I think we're here to help each other out. If we're drowning in our emotions, or just flailing about, we can grab the life preserver that is tossed our way. Then, when our feet are on solid ground, we can toss one out to someone else.

Consider a folktale I learned from family therapist Rachel Hare-Mustin.

An old man was bothered by some noisy boys playing outside his house. So he called the boys to him and told them he liked to hear them play, but he was getting deaf. If they would come over and play noisily every day, he would give each of them a quarter.

The next day they played noisily and the old man paid them. But the day after that, he gave each boy only fifteen cents, explaining that he was running out of money. The following day he said he regretted he would have to reduce the payment to five cents. The boys became angry and refused to come back because it was not worth the effort to play noisily for only five cents a day.

What a clever guy! When we feel most frustrated we're least likely to be flexible and creative—but this story reminds me that even when we are convinced that we've "tried everything," there is always something new to do after all.

I hope *Life Preservers* will help you see old problems from a new angle. It's a book to help you to stay afloat in troubled times, and buoy you up when life takes a difficult and unexpected turn. We all feel better when we have a clear direction, a solid plan, a larger and more balanced view.

Life Preservers covers the landscapes of work and creativity, anger and intimacy, friendship and marriage, children and parents, loss and betrayal, and sexuality and health. From the countless questions I have received from women over many years, I've selected those most frequently asked, as well as those rarely voiced.

Most of the questions and answers have been published in my monthly *New Woman* magazine column,

"Harriet Lerner's Good Advice" and others have never before seen print. I have received the majority of questions through the mail and each has been condensed into a paragraph. Brevity is a challenge at both ends, especially mine. It's a tall order to respond concisely to a complex problem shared in good faith by someone I have never met. I identify with the author who told a friend, "I would have written less, but I didn't have the time." It is, indeed, harder to say less.

So here are short answers to some of life's big questions. The question-and-answer format of *Life Preservers* has given me an opportunity to address the broadest range of human dilemmas—and for readers to hear my views on just about everything. I trust that women (men, too) will find themselves in these pages, take what's useful, run with it, and ignore the rest.

What we think is most shameful and unique about ourselves is often what is most universal. It helps to hear of other people's struggles and to recognize that humans are more alike than different. I want to thank all the women and men who have responded to my work with overwhelming gratitude—and more questions. The generous and inquiring letters from my readers are a life preserver for me.

1

≈

Mr. Right and Mr. Wrong

Introduction

By the time I started graduate school in the sixties, I had a vivid image of the man I was looking for. He was tall and thin, with dark, curly hair and intense brown eyes. He rode a racing bike to classes at Columbia University, where he majored in psychology or English literature, and he worked, in his spare time, for nuclear disarmament. He played guitar and flute, and wrote poetry, which he read aloud to me at night. Both in and out of bed he moved with perfect ease and grace. He was passionate and restrained, funny and serious, intellectual and unpretentious. He knew how to fix things that broke and how to tie good knots on packages. We would live together for two years in a loft in Greenwich Village after which time we would marry. Shortly thereafter he would publish his first book, which he would dedicate to me, his wife.

Though some may not have quite such a detailed picture of their ideal partner, we all know pretty much what we're looking for. Just ask us—or check the personal ads in the local paper. While individual taste varies, we want a partner who is mature and intelligent, loyal and trustworthy, loving and attentive, sensitive and open, kind and nurturant, competent and responsible. I've yet to meet a woman who says, "Well, to be honest, I'm hoping to find an irresponsible, distant, ill-tempered sort of guy who sulks a lot and won't pick up after himself."

But the kind of person we *say* we want, and who we're actually drawn to or settle for, are different matters entirely. Few of us evaluate a prospective partner with the same objectivity and clarity that we might use to select a household appliance or a car. Too many unconscious factors get in the way. One of the most powerful influences on our choice of a mate is our experience in our first family—including the quality of our parents' relationships to each other, to us, and to their own family of origin. We are also deeply affected by gender roles—the specific meanings attached to being male or female that have evolved over many generations in our particular family, class, and ethnic group.

Timing is an issue as well. We're prone to fall mindlessly in love at difficult emotional junctures—on the heels of an important loss, for example—when we're least likely to think clearly. Or we may compromise too much in a relationship or dissipate our energy trying to change him, having been taught that *any* man is better than no man at all. Moreover, it's almost impossible to imagine what intimate relationships with men—or women—would look like in a different world of true gender equality.

Historically speaking, women have learned to sacrifice the "I" for the "we" just as men have been encouraged to do the opposite, to bolster the "I" at the expense of nurturing the growth of other family members. Many women still end up in relationships where their wants, beliefs, priorities, and ambitions are compromised under relationship pressures. Of course, all relationships require flexibility and give-and-take; we don't always get what we want. But a problem arises when we do more than our 50 percent of giving in and going along.

Believing that relationships with men are supposed to be the source of their greatest joy and fulfillment, many women struggle terribly when these relationships all too frequently become a source of pain and disappointment. Women still tell me that they love too much, or not enough, or in the wrong way, or with a poorly chosen partner. The majority of letters I receive are from women seeking intimacy in unhappy relationships with men.

But intimacy won't happen if we relentlessly pressure the other person to join us in pursuing it. Nor can we make ourselves happy and secure by trying to shape him into Mr. Right. The best way to work on an intimate relationship is to work on the self. We can learn to think (rather than react) at intense times, to observe our own part in relationship patterns that keep us stuck, and to generate new options for our own behavior when the old ones aren't working.

All relationships are laboratories in which we can solve problems, engage in bold and courageous acts of change, and work toward defining ourselves. Even small steps in this direction will allow us to know ourselves and our partners better, a worthwhile venture whether we stay together over the long haul or move on.

My Boyfriend Won't Talk About Problems

Dear Harriet:

When I'm afraid or upset, I need to talk about it and analyze the problem. My boyfriend of six months, Ty, is just the opposite, though. When he's upset he doesn't dwell on it. He goes to the movies, reads a book, or goes bowling. I think Ty avoids his feelings. Ty thinks I make things worse by analyzing everything to death. I know this is a common difference between men and women. But aren't I right?

Dear Reader:

There is no "right way" to manage our feelings. When stress hits, some people seek togetherness while others seek distance; some people disclose while others are more private; some value therapy while others are do-it-yourselfers; some seek meaning while others seek relief.

People have different styles of dealing with their emotions, and differences don't mean that one person is right and the other is wrong. Think carefully about how *you* handle stress. Do you know when analyzing your problems is helpful and when it's not? When dwelling on your problems gets you nowhere, can you distract yourself and go bowling?

Ty may also want to think about his style of managing stress. Does distracting himself always work? What are the costs? Can he be emotionally present and simply listen when you need to talk with him, even if talking isn't "his way"?

Of course, every style of managing stress, no matter how useful, has a potential down side. Reflection can turn into rumination—a focus on the negative that draws us deeper into it. Distracting ourselves from pain can turn into an entrenched pattern of avoidance, denial, and emotional detachment. Each of us is the best judge of when our response to pain diminishes or adds to it.

We fare best when we are honest observers of ourselves, and when we use our creativity and flexibility to generate new solutions to old problems. If what we are doing isn't working, it won't help to do more of the same—be it bowling or introspecting. Nor is it good to have only one way to respond to pain. If *all* we can do is focus on our problems—or *all* we can do is distract ourselves from them—then we're likely to get stuck.

> When stress hits, some people seek togetherness while others seek distance.

In time, you may come to appreciate the differences between you and Ty; each of you might even benefit from becoming a bit more like the other. Or, alternately, you may decide that it's important for you to be with someone who, like yourself, values self-revelation, personal sharing, and conversation about difficult emotional issues. Try to get clear about this so you don't end up staying in a compromising relationship, or one where you dissipate your energies trying to change your partner.

Is He Having an Affair?

Dear Harriet:

I'm a thirty-year-old successful executive, frantically worried that my fiancé, Warren, is having an affair. I've confronted him repeatedly with my suspicions, and he insists that it's all in my head. But I sense that he is distant and just not "there." I have two married friends who have hired private detectives in similar circumstances without their husbands' knowledge. They insist I should do the same. What would you do?

Dear Reader:

If I felt so distrustful of another human being as to consider having him investigated, I wouldn't be setting a marriage date. I probably wouldn't even use that person to feed my cat when I left town. I would put marriage plans on hold and take whatever time I needed to gain more clarity about the level of intimacy, honesty, and trust in the relationship.

If I hired a private investigator, I would feel as if I were the one having the affair. If I introduced this level of secrecy and deception into a relationship, I would find it difficult to restore intimacy, to say nothing of self-regard. I would not want to respond to mistrust by becoming untrustworthy and secretive myself.

Consider how you would respond if Warren invaded your privacy. If he believed you were concealing information from him, would it be OK for him to tap your phone, bug your office, open your mail, or hire someone to trail you? Would you respect Warren's "right to know" by whatever means possible—or might you feel violated, betrayed, or intruded upon? Work toward clarifying your values so that whatever actions you take to allay your suspicions reflect your ethics and beliefs—not just your fears.

Trust your intuition that something is wrong, but consider another option: try approaching Warren without anger, intensity, or accusations. Let him know that you love him but that you have been unable to discount your sense that something is going on. You might say, for example, "Warren, I feel that something has changed in our relationship. You keep telling me it's all in my head, but my feeling that something is wrong isn't going away."

Share your concerns with Warren without blaming him: "Warren, when I feel you aren't emotionally present, I worry without knowing what to think. I wonder if you're having an affair or if you're in trouble at work or if you have a health problem or if you're questioning our engagement. Whatever it is, I want us to be able to talk about it. The hardest thing for me is to sense so strongly that something is wrong and to be told that I'm just imagining it."

> We can't prevent other people from lying to us, whether through their words or their silence.

Meanwhile, do your best to calm your emotions. The higher our level of anxiety, the less accurately we perceive and process information. Fear propels us to overreact and to read too much into things or to underreact and ignore what is before our eyes. Anxiety drives us to extremes.

Take as much time as you need to deepen your knowledge of Warren and to restore your level of comfort. How well do you know his family and friends? What questions have you asked him about his past relationships? What's his track record when it comes to honesty and fidelity? Is he usually open or closed about difficult emotional issues in his life? And do you consider *yourself* to be a jealous person? We don't need a detective to learn more about a person over time. Most important, if you don't trust Warren to tell you the truth, don't marry him.

Try as we may to "read" people accurately, we can't prevent other people from lying to us, whether through their words or their silence. Nor can we know when they are telling us the whole truth. We can, however, stay as aware as possible and try to live our own lives authentically, truly, and honorably. In my mind, hiring a private investigator is not a step in this direction.

What Is Intimacy?

Dear Harriet:

I'm dating a man, Rob, whom I feel passionate about. I think about him constantly and I'm not exaggerating. I know he is rude, distant, and selfish, but that doesn't dampen my feelings for him. My friends say passion is not the same as true intimacy, and they want me to break it off. What is true intimacy? What causes this incredible passion I feel for Rob, and how do I get my friends to stop pressuring me to leave him?

Dear Reader:

Intimacy is a large word. No single definition fits all its forms. From my perspective, intimacy requires mutuality, which means mutual valuing, mutual empowerment, mutual respect, and mutual empathy. A truly intimate relationship fosters the growth of both parties, not just one.

Psychiatrist Jean Baker Miller identifies five "good things" that occur within a growth-fostering relationship, or even within a growth-fostering conversation:

1. Each person feels a greater sense of "zest" (vitality and energy).

2. Each person feels more able to act and does act.

3. Each person has a more accurate picture of herself or himself and of the other person.

4. Each person feels a greater sense of worth.

5. Each person feels more connected to the other per-

son and feels a greater motivation for connections with other people beyond those in the specific relationship.

Consider whether these things are present or absent in your interactions with Rob, and whether they were there to begin with.

You might want to consider why your attachment to Rob is so intense. Intensity is not the same as intimacy, although we tend to confuse these two words. Intense feelings, rather than being a measure of true and enduring closeness, may block us from taking a careful and objective look at our partner, ourselves, and the dance we're doing together. And intense togetherness can easily flip into intense distance, or intense conflict, for that matter.

No one knows what causes the sort of passion you describe, although we do know that it blurs clear thinking and can lead us to distance ourselves from our friends and even abandon our life plan for someone we wouldn't even choose for a roommate. But you don't owe anyone an apology for staying with him. Over time you can sort out what this relationship means to you and what it can teach you.

In the meantime, if you want your friends to back off, tell them so. People in the grip of passion don't heed the advice of friends (or experts) anyway. But do think about

> Intensity is not the same as intimacy, although we tend to confuse these two words.

where your relationship with Rob will be five years down the road if you continue with your "anything goes" policy. The risk is that you may end up sacrificing both your relationship and your self-regard.

Why Can't I Find Mr. Right?

Dear Harriet:

I'm a happy, productive, and successful single woman in her late forties who would very much like to remarry. (My first husband divorced me eight years ago.) The problem is that "Mr. Right" has just not come along. I've read several inspirational and self-help books that say when a woman is ready, the right man will arrive. Does the fact that I'm still single mean that I have problems with intimacy that require professional help?

Dear Reader:

Many popular books falsely imply that if only we would overcome our personal conflicts—and behave in the right way—we would have no problem finding and keeping a man. Yes, there he'd be, gals, waiting in the corridor, or coming out of the woodwork, ready for intimacy! We're apt to blame ourselves, rather than these books, when he fails to show up.

Psychotherapy can help you address conflicts with intimacy (we all have them), but no amount of hard work will guarantee that "Mr. Right" will appear. Nor does your single status indicate a problem. The old adage "A good man is hard to find" is true, as you know from experience. It becomes even truer as we get older, more settled, more successful, and rightfully fussier.

> Finding the right man is a matter of emotional readiness—but it's also a matter of opportunity, effort, and, yes, luck.

You're the best judge of whether you have problems of your own that might stand in your way. If Mr. Right magically appeared at your door tomorrow, would anything block you from getting off to a good start? Would there be something in the way of achieving greater intimacy over time? What in your history with men gives you reason to be concerned?

Do the obvious. Maximize any opportunities to meet people. And remind your friends that you want their help introducing you to suitable men. As for therapy, finding the right man is partly a matter of emotional readiness—but it's also a matter of opportunity, effort, and, yes, luck.

Is He the One?

Dear Harriet:

I'm madly in love with a man named Tom who is thirty-seven years old and has been divorced three times. My best friend is telling me to drop him right now or I'll become divorce number four. Is my friend right? Should you choose a partner with your heart or your head?

Dear Reader:

Choosing an intimate partner is surely a task of the heart, which involves feelings, desire, and intuition. Few of us first compile a list of important qualities and then proceed with the selection process. Picking a partner is not like choosing a job candidate.

We would all do well, however, to combine our feelings and intuition with observation and thought. We might even seriously consider the job-application approach and take a hard look at a person's track record in navigating relationships. Many women put more careful judgment into selecting a new toaster oven than they put into evaluating a prospective partner.

Take your time and draw upon *both* your intellect and emotions. Steamy starts are compelling, but the more you can slow down and stay clearheaded, the better your chances of gathering a more objective picture of Tom. In addition, be careful not to insulate this important relationship from your other relationships. You'll learn most about Tom if you observe him among both *your* friends and family and *his.*

Talk openly and directly with Tom about the key people in his life. Does he blame his previous wives or their families for marital difficulties, or does he take responsibility as well? How did each of these marriages end? (If he says that wife number one was needy and infantile, wife number two was exploitative and manipulative, and wife number three was an all-around neurotic bitch—well, watch out.) What about Tom's relationships with his parents, siblings, and friends: are they calm and connected or distant and blaming?

> Many women put more careful judgment
> into selecting a new appliance than
> they put into evaluating a mate.

Should any one fact or combination of facts make you cross Tom off your list? This is a decision only you can make, and without a crystal ball, no one can say for sure what the future will bring for the two of you. Do give yourself plenty of time to consider all information, both intuitive and objective.

My Fiancé Has a Violent Temper

Dear Harriet:

I am engaged to a man named Sam who is generous, loving, and considerate. However, he has a violent temper. He sometimes throws furniture around, and once he slammed his fist into a wall. This makes me very nervous. Is it possible that he might one day hit me?

Dear Reader:

Sam *may* hit you some day. Any man who is out of control during the engagement stage of a relationship may become more out of control in the future. Marriage is like a lightning rod, absorbing tensions from every source. Add children, or simply the inevitable stresses of the life cycle, and Sam's violent temper may well intensify. In a society where every statistic on violence against women has soared in the past two decades, you have good reason to be nervous.

On the other hand, Sam may never hit you. Even the most logical and careful predictions are sometimes wrong. No one can say with absolute certainty if—or when—Sam will hit you.

Have you talked to Sam about your concerns? If not, pick a calm time and question him directly. Has he ever hit anyone? Is there a history of violence in his family? Does Sam think he would ever hurt you in the future? On a scale of one to ten, how likely is that to occur? Open the lines of communication by sharing your concerns and by asking clear and specific questions.

Let Sam know that you are terrified of violence and

that you cannot live with it. Or can you? You need to direct some tough questions to yourself, not just to Sam. Being "very nervous" about violence, or even detesting it, is a far cry from defining a clear position about it. You can't predict or control Sam's behavior, not now or ever. What you can control is your own position regarding his behavior.

What aggressive behaviors can you live with despite your dislike of them? What behaviors are intolerable in a relationship? In other words, what is your bottom-line position about violence? ("Sam, I cannot stay in this relationship if you throw one more thing and don't get help with the problem.")

Keep in mind that there is no "right" bottom line for all women. One woman might break off an engagement the very first time her fiancé threw furniture or slammed his fist into a wall. Or she might end the relationship if such out-of-control behavior occurred several times and he wouldn't seek help. Another woman might wait until she had been struck twice—or twelve times—before she said, "Enough!" Another might complain or issue angry ultimatums but never leave, no matter what.

Where are you on this continuum? What position have you taken so far? Keep in mind that when our words say one thing ("I can't live with this!") and our actions say another (we continue to live with it), actions speak louder.

If you have difficulty being clear with yourself, or being heard by Sam, you should talk openly about your problem to a few close friends and family members. Have other women on your family tree (including sisters, aunts, and grandmothers) maintained clear positions on such matters in their marriages? How would they react to the out-of-control behaviors you describe? Has anyone stayed in an emotionally or physically abusive marriage? The more you know about the patterns in your family, the more clearly you will think about your own dilemma and the family and cultural patterns that relate to your struggle.

This is not to say that when violence escalates you are ever "to blame" or "the cause." You are not. Our culture excuses and even glorifies expressions of violence and aggression in men while teaching women not to take action on our own behalf. Historically, women have been

> Marriage is like a lightning rod,
> absorbing tensions from every source.

considered the chattel of men; only relatively recently has spouse abuse been prosecuted.

While the blame isn't yours, change occurs only when we focus on the self and take a new position on our own behalf. You could say, for example, "Sam, the next time you throw something or lose control I will leave immediately because I get scared and upset. I'll return the next day if you've calmed down. But if it happens more than once, I will not come back at all until you get help and get a handle on it."

Obviously, you can set limits with Sam only *after* you have defined them for yourself. This may take time, and I encourage you to take all the time you need before you tie the knot. Imagine how much more difficult it is to clarify a bottom line when you're, say, a middle-aged homemaker with three dependent children and no marketable skills— or you have a husband who threatens to hurt you if you leave. And postponing a wedding date now is less emotionally complicated than filing for divorce later.

Marriage often puts women in a position of profound emotional and economic vulnerability. Take care now to make a life plan for yourself that will enable you to live your life as well as possible, with or without Sam. This will help you clarify—and really stand by—your position regarding Sam's violent behaviors.

Should I Lie to Keep Him?

Dear Harriet:

I have herpes but only experience occasional break-outs. Every time I do the right thing and reveal this to a guy I want to develop a relationship with, he bolts. I think it's only fair to share this information right up front, but I'm despairing of ever finding a man who will stick around past the first date. Should I lie?

Dear Reader:

If a prospective partner bolts in response to your well-meaning revelation that you have herpes, what does that say about him as a person? If a man truly values you, he'll stick around, herpes or not.

Dishonesty is not the solution, because it occurs at your partner's expense as well as your own. Lying is hardly the way to build a solid foundation for a relationship. Moreover, when he eventually finds out the truth, he'll be more angry still. Instead, try to get to know each other before jumping into bed and sharing your health history. Consider developing a nonsexual relationship first—even if it takes several weeks or months. The problem of herpes will become less important as your relationship develops.

How do we reveal sensitive material to a new partner or friend? The subject may be a health diagnosis, infertility, a financial problem, or any event in our history or family that we consider shameful. The goal is not to "tell all" right up front, but rather to consider matters of timing and tact so that we can widen the space for honesty and truth-telling as the relationship deepens.

He Won't Commit

Dear Harriet:

A decade ago my disastrous marriage ended in divorce. Then, several years ago, I met my dream man, Jim. I was eager for marriage, and he agreed but insisted that we live together first. The problem is he's still avoiding setting the date. The more I pressure him, the more he distances himself from me. Marriage is my first priority, but two years of pursuing Jim and neglecting everything else haven't worked. What else can I do?

Dear Reader:

We all have mixed emotions about getting married. But sometimes one partner (often, but not always, the woman) expresses all the positive feelings while the other partner (often, but not always, the man) expresses all the negative ones.

Under stress, women often seek more togetherness; men, more distance. Neither response is inherently a problem, but the pattern that's set in motion can be. The more the woman pursues, the more the man distances. The more he distances, the more she pursues. This means that if you continue to pursue Jim for a commitment, he will continue to dig in his heels.

Pursuers *protect* distancers. As long as one person pursues, the other has the luxury of experiencing a cool independence and a need for space. If one expresses all the dependency and neediness, the other can disown these qualities. When a pursuer can back off and concentrate on her own life—especially if she can do this with dignity, zest, and without anger—the distancer is more likely to recognize his own needs for closeness and commitment.

Since pursuing Jim is not working, consider a bold and courageous experiment. Set aside a realistic amount of time—say, eight weeks—to change your steps in the old dance. During this period, stop focusing on Jim and put your energy back into your work, your friends, and your own life plan. Stay warmly connected to Jim (that is, don't swing into a cold, reactive distance), but don't pursue him or talk about your desire to get married.

Instead, share your own concerns about marriage with Jim. (Yes, we all have them.) For example: "Jim, I want to apologize for being on your case about getting married. I've been acting as if I'm sure it's the right thing. But my first marriage was a disaster, and part of me is scared to do it again. I've been letting you express all the ambivalence, but I have mixed feelings myself."

If you're a "natural" pursuer, it will be difficult for you to change your behavior. And because my advice may smack of the old "hard-to-get" tactics that women have been taught to use, it may sound manipulative. But there is no virtue in continuing with the status quo. Polarized relationships (she stands for togetherness, he for distance) distort the experience of both partners and succeed only in keeping us stuck.

What happens if you break the pattern of pursuit and distance, and nothing changes? Clarify your priorities. Is your first priority to be married, even at the expense of losing Jim? If so, take a firm bottom-line position. Pick a calm time and talk with Jim about how long you can wait for him to make a decision. ("Jim, I love you and I want to spend my life with you. But marriage is so important to me that I can't continue to live with you without a commitment. I know you need more time to make a decision, but let's decide on how *much* time.") Be clear about your own

limits. ("I can wait another ten months while you're deciding what's best for you, but if you're still unsure, I'm going
to move on, as painful as that will be for me.")

However, don't take a bottom-line position at a time
when you're feeling anxious, blaming, or otherwise
intense. Nor should it be
issued as a threat, an ultimatum, or an attempt to rope
Jim in. Rather, a bottom-line
position is a calm, nonblaming clarification of the limits
of what is acceptable or tolerable in a relationship.

> Stop focusing on
> whether he'll marry
> you, and put your
> energy back into
> your own life plan.

If you take such a posi-
tion, give Jim lots of space during the waiting period. Try
to *under*react—rather than *over*react—to his expressions of
ambivalence and doubt. This will give Jim the emotional
space to struggle with his dilemma and give your relationship its best chance of succeeding.

If, however, your first priority is to preserve your relationship with Jim, consider lightening up about marriage
for an indefinite period of time. Enjoy your time together,
whether or not you marry. You know from your first experience that marriage does not ensure security or happiness.
Moreover, if you let go of your focus on marriage as an end
in and of itself, you and Jim will be able to view the positives
and negatives of your relationship more objectively.

Remember, focusing on your own life is good advice,
whether or not you marry Jim. Focusing on a relationship
at the expense of personal goals isn't fair to you and risks
overloading the relationship. The best way to work on your
relationship with Jim is to work on yourself.

I Always Pick the Wrong Guys

Dear Harriet:

I always fall for men who are unsuitable partners. My current boyfriend is mean, selfish, and irresponsible. Several of my girlfriends married total jerks, and I'm afraid I'll do the same. Why do intelligent women stay with jerks and waste time trying to change them? What's the psychological scoop on this pattern?

Dear Reader:

Here are a few theories, all of which—or none of which—may fit.

Low self-esteem may lead a woman to feel that she deserves no better than a "lousy guy." Furthermore, her own sense of worth may be enhanced by pairing with a man who can be criticized or "saved" rather than admired.

If her own parents' marriage was unhappy or ungratifying, the woman may unconsciously feel disloyal should she forge a new, more gratifying pattern. And if one of her parents was deemed unsuitable or incompetent by the other, she may repeat the family pattern in an unconscious attempt, however doomed, to make an old painful scenario end differently.

Living with a "jerk" can also allow one the luxury of putting enormous energy into endless cycles of fighting, accusation, and blame, directed toward the person one believes to be responsible for one's own unhappiness. In this way, a woman can avoid the more difficult task of assuming responsibility for the quality and direction of her own life.

Some women stay with unsuitable guys because we internalize the social dictate that "half a loaf is better than none" (i.e., *any* man is better than no man). True enough, single women no longer have the devalued status that they once did. (When I was growing up, the difference between a "bachelor" and an "old maid" was all too clear.) Yet our society still does not accord equal value and respect to women without male partners.

Some women believe that *any* man
is better than no man at all.

To gain insight into your own choices, you might do well to learn about the marriages of your relatives. What patterns can you discern? Which marriages, if any, approximate what you would like for yourself? Are there marriages in which both partners view themselves and each other with love and respect?

Your friends and family can serve as resources to help you. Psychotherapy may help, too. But we don't always need to analyze or understand something to change it. You may one day gather the strength to walk away from a "jerk"—even if you don't know what drew you to him in the first place.

He Won't Wear a Condom

Dear Harriet:

I've just begun dating Stan, an incredible guy. Unfortunately, he says condoms ruin his experience of sex and that he only enjoys making love when he performs *au naturel.* I'm afraid I'll lose him if I insist on condoms or even bring the subject up. Stan also says that women are overreacting to the AIDS scare and that I can use a spermicide for safe sex. I never meet brilliant and creative men like Stan, and I want to please him. Is there much risk of AIDS if I'm not promiscuous and Stan is a very selective guy?

Dear Reader:

Women have a long tradition of pleasing men and sacrificing the self in relationships. But you are speaking here of a very large sacrifice: your life.

Of what value are Stan's "brilliance" and "creativity" if he has no room in his heart to consider you? And why would you choose to be complicitous with behaviors that put your life at risk?

Is the risk minimal? I'm afraid not. There has been widespread denial of the threat of AIDS to women, a denial that is part of a broader picture of inadequate attention to and research funding for women's health concerns. Women, as a group, are in danger of *under*reacting, not *over*reacting, to the critical threat of AIDS. Over the past decade the incidence of AIDS among women in the United States has more than doubled, from 7 percent of all new cases in 1985 to 18 percent in 1994, and AIDS is still on the rise. Minorities of both sexes are especially hard hit.

Investigative reporter Gena Corea reveals that it is at least ten times more likely that a man will transmit the virus to a woman during sex than the other way around, yet many men refuse to wear condoms. Every woman is at risk for HIV/AIDS, including women with one or few sexual partners. AIDS in not a disease that strikes "bad" or "promiscuous" women. The 1990 Brown University AIDS Program Study of ninety heterosexual women with HIV found that the median number of long-term sexual partners for each of them was only three.

Stan is also misinformed about spermicide blocking viral infection. Nonoxynol-9 is the only spermicide that has been tested for viricidal qualities. And while it may have some benefit when used with condoms, Nonoxynol-9 alone was found unsuitable for HIV prevention. Only latex condoms, for oral sex as well as intercourse, have proved effective in guarding against HIV. Of course, truly safe sex demands that a couple get an AIDS test. After receiving negative results, they must then be abstinent or have protected, monogamous sex for six months and then get retested. After a second set of negative results—and remaining monogamous—it is generally accepted that the couple is HIV-negative.

It may be excruciatingly difficult to say "Let's talk about condoms" and risk facing Stan's anger, disapproval, and rejection. But I hope you will let Stan know that you're afraid and that you won't consider having unprotected sex.

Stan's response to your insistence that you count will tell you a great deal about his character, values, and regard for you. This important information about a prospective partner is better known earlier rather that later in a relationship. If you and Stan care for each other, you can find a way to be physically intimate that considers both of your needs and safety as much as possible. A solid and mature partner will compromise his desires rather than invite you to compromise your life.

No matter how many verbal assurances a prospective sexual partner might make, no woman should voluntarily engage in unprotected sex on a date. Men may lie to women about their sexual history in order to get them to bed. Asking men questions about their sexual and drug history is unquestionably a good idea, but it's hardly a prevention against AIDS. It is wildly naive to assume that someone you have only recently met will provide you with a factual account of their sexual history.

> A solid and mature partner will compromise his desires rather than invite you to compromise your life.

It's not enough for individual women to follow the usual self-help advice (keep latex condoms in your purse, and "Just say no!"), because the problem demands larger solutions. We live in a world where women are sexually exploited, where female submission is eroticized, where sexual violence is epidemic, where women as a group lack economic power and social authority, and where women's health issues are shamefully neglected and underfunded. All this must change before any one of us can take safe sex for granted or ensure it through our individual efforts.

What If He Says No?

Dear Harriet:

I'm attracted to my neighbor Bob. I want to ask him to have lunch with me sometime, but I'm frozen by my fear of rejection. Although I've been in therapy for years, my fear of rejection has not improved. I'm lonely but too nervous to do anything about it. Any advice about Bob?

Dear Reader:

No one enjoys being turned down. But if you choose to live courageously, you will experience, and survive, many rejections. The only sure way to avoid rejection is to sit mute in a corner and take no risks.

If you wait until you are analyzed, therapized, or unafraid, you may be waiting too long. As the late poet Audre Lorde wrote, "I realize that if I wait until I am no longer afraid to act, write, speak, be, I'll be sending messages on a Ouija board, cryptic complaints from the other side."

If a negative response from Bob would be too much for you at this time, you don't have to push yourself. You can do nothing—or you can test out the waters with Bob by more overt friendliness and contact. Respect your own sense of timing. Whatever you decide about Bob, the real challenge is the long-term one of moving in the direction of more courage and connection over time.

> The only sure way to avoid rejection is to sit mute in a corner and take no risks.

My Fiancé Collects Pornography

Dear Harriet:

My fiancé, Dean, has a huge stash of porno magazines and adult movies under his bed that he doesn't know I have seen. I am planning to move in with him next month, and our wedding date is set for the summer. The pictures in his pornography collection are so degrading to women that I don't think I can handle it. I can't tell him to get rid of it, because I know he won't. I can't even mention it to him, because we will end up in a fight. Is his interest in porno normal behavior for a man? Am I wrong to disapprove? Do I have a problem?

Dear Reader:

The pornography you describe may be "normal" (that is, the norm in our society), but that doesn't mean it's good for anyone. You have every right to feel upset about Dean's collection. Of course, Dean, too, has a right to his beliefs on the subject of pornography.

Yes, you do have a problem. Your problem is not that you disapprove of Dean's pornography collection but rather that you have not found a way to talk with him about it. Dealing openly and directly with our differences is a central challenge in all intimate relationships, and it's never easy. You seem convinced that you must suppress your feelings and keep quiet to preserve the peace. But if you do, you won't have much of a marriage. More important, you won't have much of a self.

You can't make Dean relinquish his pornography collection, nor can you convince him to see things your way.

It's not our job to change or fix our partner, nor is doing so even possible. It *is* our job, however, to be honest in all our relationships. If you're not able to be up front with your feelings now, where will you and Dean be five or ten years from now? Marriage makes it harder, not easier, to clarify the "I" within the "we."

Pornography aside, how well do you and Dean meet the challenge of dealing openly and respectfully with your differences? Have you talked with Dean about your expectations of marriage and your own tendency to silence yourself to avoid conflict?

If you are feeling brave, pick a calm time to share your feelings with Dean about his pornography collection. If you can clearly articulate your reactions—without anger or blame—you will learn more about Dean's willingness to respect and consider your feelings. If you feel that the pornography issue is too difficult to address calmly just yet, try asserting yourself first in another area that is less emotionally loaded.

> Your problem is not the pornography
> collection but that you have not found
> a way to talk about it.

In the meantime, consider putting on hold your plans to move in together and marry. It may seem like a big risk to take right now, but until you feel comfortable talking openly and honestly with Dean about your feelings, marriage is a much bigger one.

He Wants to See Other People

Dear Harriet:

I'm twenty-eight years old and eager to settle down. For the past three months I've been dating Louis, a man my age, who is the first guy I've met in a long time that I would consider as a lifetime partner. The problem is that he's seeing another woman and says he's not ready to choose. I want this relationship to work, and don't want to lose him, but sometimes it seems impossible to continue this way. Do I threaten to break up with him, or is there another way?

Dear Reader:

Some women in your situation could calmly adopt a wait-and-see attitude over a considerable time. Others would tell Louis to make a choice. It's not a matter of right or wrong; your decision should reflect your own values and beliefs as well as your level of comfort with maintaining the status quo.

Pay attention to how you're feeling. Persistent anger or other distress may be a signal that you can't continue in the current situation; it's not healthy for you, and it can't be good for your relationship. If you're feeling deeply unhappy, you might tell Louis that the situation isn't workable for you, that you need to move on with your life and keep your eyes open for a good monogamous relationship. You can tell Louis to call you if and when the time comes that he's not involved with anyone else. Let him know, however, that you don't plan to put your life on hold.

Before taking action, though, learn as much as possible about Louis to help you make a thoughtful decision. How long has he been dating this other woman—five years or five months? What's his pattern of navigating previous relationships? (Does he tend to have more than one partner at a time? What has been the outcome?) Would he feel comfortable dating two women over the next several years, or does he, too, eventually want to settle down?

No single bit of information is reason enough to end a relationship, but it's all part of knowing Louis better and making a more informed decision. Question yourself, as well. Do you have a pattern of getting involved with men who are unavailable, or who otherwise can't meet your needs.

Consider all your options, including dating Louis without having sex. Remember that you will have the best chance of resolving the issue if you can decide what's best for you and take a position without anger or blame. It's good that Louis is straightforward with you about his sexual behavior and his affections. Keep in mind that he's more likely

> Persistent anger or other distress may be a signal that you can't continue in the current situation.

to be in touch with how much he wants you (or doesn't) if you're not pursuing or pressuring him.

My Boyfriend Isn't Generous

Dear Harriet:

I'm in a serious relationship with a man who makes about the same amount of money I do. Don always insists that we split the cost of our dates fifty-fifty. Most of the time I'm happy to pay my own way, but once in a while it would be nice to have him treat me. It might seem petty, but I'm worried that his unwillingness to pick up the occasional tab indicates a lack of generosity on his part that doesn't bode well for our future together. Am I right to be concerned?

Dear Reader:

Money is a "high twitch" subject for many people. Few folks are objective about it. Attitudes about money are passed down through the generations, and our personal views on the subject are shaped by the struggles of family members who came before us. It might help to place Don's fifty-fifty position—and your reactions to it—in a broader family context.

For example, has Don (or any member of his family) ever been taken advantage of financially by a partner in love or work? Has economic survival—or financial inequality between spouses—been a concern to anyone in his family in the past? How do beliefs and behaviors about spending and sharing money differ between your family

> If he became the primary wage earner, would he consider the money more rightfully his to control?

and his? And finally, how does Don imagine your relationship might change if one of you made more money and picked up the tab, say, 90 percent of the time?

Remember that you and Don are two different people who come together with separate family legacies about spending. There's no reason why you two should think and feel the same way about who contributes what. Instead, what's important is that you talk to each other openly and respectfully about your differences.

Is Don generous in other areas? The only way to find out is by getting to know him—and yourself—better. Determine what specific acts of generosity are important to you, then put Don to the test.

Do you have a particular worry about the future? Are you concerned, for example, that if you and Don married and he became the primary wage earner after a baby came, he would consider the money more rightfully his to control? Address your concerns directly with Don.

Meanwhile, since you and Don do earn approximately the same amount, there's no reason you can't start the ball rolling by exhibiting your own generosity. On your next date, consider taking the initiative and treating Don. If he really believes in sharing everything half and half, he'll probably want to treat you in return.

Should I Move In with Him?

Dear Harriet:

My boyfriend, Kurt, and I are contemplating marriage. To be honest, I'm not sure he's right for me. Now he
wants me to move in with him in order to speed up my
decision. He says he will support me if we live together,
and I can't help feeling tempted since he owns a fantastic
place. What would you do in my situation? Will living with
him help me decide whether to marry him?

Dear Reader:

Living with Kurt will give you an opportunity to get to
know him better. Many couples who marry—or ultimately
choose not to—are glad they lived together first.

Living together, however, can also blur your clarity.
Once you've settled in with Kurt, you may find it hard to

> Living together will give you new
> information—but so will spending
> six weeks entirely apart.

move out, even if that is the wiser choice in the long run.
You are especially vulnerable if there is a great economic
disparity between you two. Like our fairy-tale heroines,
many of us wish for a man who will transform us from
scullery maid to princess, even if the relationship itself is
compromised.

If you're not sure about marrying Kurt, the proximity of living together will give you new information—but so will, say, spending six weeks entirely apart. The more you become economically dependent on Kurt, the less clarity you may have about your relationship and—as is often the case for women—about marriage itself.

What would I do in your place? If I wanted to marry Kurt, I would live with him first. If I had any significant doubts, I would stay put in my own apartment. But this is your decision, which should reflect your deepest values, priorities, and desires, along with your best thinking. No one else can determine what's right or best for you.

Do I Take His Last Name?

Dear Harriet:

I've always believed that women should retain their birth-given last name in marriage. But now that I'm about to marry a man with a simple last name, I'm thinking of taking it, because my last name is long and hard to spell. My fiancé, Bruce, says I shouldn't worry that taking his name will make me a less independent person. He says the naming issue has nothing to do with equality and is "much ado about nothing." What's your opinion?

Dear Reader:

Men know that naming is much ado about *something*, even when they pretend otherwise. How many men do you know who have traded in their name for a spouse's because her name was easier? Or prettier? Or for any other reason, for that matter? (I know one such man.) Giving up one's name, or *keeping* one's name but not giving it to off-spring, is not a small matter for at least half of our species.

I agree with Bruce that taking his name won't make you a less independent person. But your individual dilemma takes place in a larger social context of inequality. An individual black person is not diminished by choosing to sit at the back of the bus, but when a decision about who sits where (like a decision about who takes whose name) is made on the basis of race or gender, it reflects institution-alized inequality. And it matters a great deal.

Which is not to instill guilt if you change your name. I can identify entirely with your dilemma. When I married in 1971, I transformed myself from Harriet Goldhor (pronounced Goldhoar) to Harriet Lerner with a great sense of relief. The last syllable of my name evoked merciless teasing during my adolescence (a neighborhood boy called me "Henrietta Whorehead," and "Silverslut" was a later variation on the same theme), and I felt uncomfortable when introduced to new people who would invariably say, "Gold-what?" To be honest, "Lerner" is still a relief, but I have mixed feelings to this day about my decision.

> Men know that naming matters a great deal, even when they pretend otherwise.

I have admittedly poor credentials from which to advise you. Every woman's decision, if it reflects her values and beliefs, deserves our respect. But whatever our personal choice, I hope none of us will pretend that naming doesn't matter.

My Boyfriend Is Bisexual

Dear Harriet:

I am seriously involved with a wonderful man who may be bisexual. Apart from the question of his physical health (he has been tested for the AIDS virus and the results were negative), I am concerned about his emotional health. Ken has admitted to having had several purely sexual affairs with men in the past, but says that he now wants a monogamous and committed relationship with a woman. I have difficulty understanding his true sexuality, and I wonder if I can trust his feelings for me enough to think of him as husband material.

Dear Reader:

Many well-adjusted folks are attracted to both sexes and act on that attraction. Although our culture tends to value and legitimize only heterosexual bonding, this bias is based on prejudice and fear, not reason. The fact that Ken has had affairs with men is not evidence of emotional difficulty. Just like anyone else, he may or may not have serious problems with commitment and intimacy.

At the same time, your concern about Ken's sexuality is justified, because he may be using the label of bisexuality to protect him from the emotional cost of having to own up to a primarily homosexual orientation. In wanting to commit to a woman, Ken may be making an honest effort to go the route that society dictates, but he may also be fooling himself. And if he is denying an important aspect of his own emotional and sexual orientation, it will catch up with him over time.

Take the time to get to know Ken better before making a serious commitment. Learn as much as possible about his previous relationships with both men and women—how they began, how they evolved, how long they lasted, and what Ken's track record is regarding commitment, honesty, and fidelity. And consider your own reservations about intimacy as well.

> Your boyfriend may be making an honest effort to go the route that society dictates, but he may also be fooling himself.

If Ken has had sexual relationships with other men, most likely this aspect of his sexuality is an integral part of himself that will not go away. He won't stop being attracted to men simply as a result of committing to you, and you need to confront in your own mind how you feel about this and whether you can accept it. This possibility is not a condemnation of Ken but simply something to keep in mind in contemplating the future of your relationship. No relationship comes with a guarantee, and no one enters marriage with a crystal ball. When uncertainty enters any relationship, it's a good idea to slow down, keep the lines of communication open, use your head (not just your heart), and always practice safe sex.

He Hates Spending Time with My Friends and Family

Dear Harriet:

I've been dating Andy for a year. The problem is that he won't spend any time with my friends or family. We argue about this constantly, but I can't win. He says he only wants to be with me. He won't even accept a dinner invitation. We're getting married soon, and I need to know why he's like this.

Dear Reader:

I don't know why Andy refuses to spend time with your friends and family. Perhaps Andy isn't entirely clear on this point himself. But arguing with him won't provide the missing pieces. Changing the pattern will.

You need to see Andy interacting with the important people in your life—and the important people in *his* life—both to know him better and to understand his extreme position. So be firm about your need to include friends and family during some of your time together. Don't fight or provide lengthy justifications for your point of view. Just tell Andy that it's really crucial to you that the people you love have the opportunity to get to know each other.

If Andy refuses to honor your wishes, I think you should reevaluate your wedding plans and let Andy know that the issue is so important that you can't move forward until it gets resolved. You might suggest counseling as a way to foster more communication about your differences.

Consider your own possible contributions to the problem as well; your difficulty making yourself heard, your willingness to go along with behaviors that violate your core values and beliefs, and your readiness to marry someone who is waving a big red flag in your face.

> Arguing won't provide the missing pieces.
> Changing the pattern will.

My Fiancé Doesn't Like Sex

Dear Harriet:

My fiancé, Gary, seems to have no interest in sex and never initiates sexual encounters. If I press him, he will occasionally "perform," but I can tell that he doesn't really enjoy it. He says that he has no sex drive or any wish for physical closeness. I want him to see a counselor but he refuses. He says that when we are married, things will get better. Sex is important to me, and I'm tired of pursuing him. What's causing his disinterest, and how can I bring him out of his shell?

Dear Reader:

Both men and women avoid sexual intimacy for any number of reasons, some of which may be disturbing to you but you need to consider. Gary may be depressed or he may fear closeness. Prescription drugs as well as illegal drugs can inhibit desire. Gary may not want to admit to you (or himself) that he is gay. He may be terrified of sex because of an early sexual trauma. He may have an organically based sexual dysfunction or suffer from a sexually transmitted disease. He may secretly be finding his sexual pleasure elsewhere.

The best way to handle the situation is to approach Gary without accusation or blame and ask him directly whether any or all of these factors my be contributing to his problem. It will help you to understand Gary's sexual distance if you ask him clear and specific questions: Has there ever been a time when his sex drive was livelier or when he experienced a pleasurable sexual relationship?

Can he tell you how his sexual behavior, attitudes, and values have changed over time? Does he masturbate, and if so, whom or what does he think about when he does so? Has he ever considered the possibility that he might be gay? Does he think he has a sexual problem, and what crosses his mind about having no sex drive? You

> Don't think that marriage will magically solve the problem. It won't.

don't need to have a marathon conversation in which you ask everything at once. You do need to continue the coversation over time.

There is nothing that you can do to inspire Gary's sexual interest or to solve his problem. You can, however, take a clear position that you will not marry him unless the two of you seek consultation from an expert who is skilled both in sex therapy and in couples therapy. If you continue as you have been (pursuing Gary for sex without a clear plan for working on the problem), then nothing will change.

The challenge for you is to avoid complaining about Gary, pursuing him for sex, or allowing yourself to believe that marriage will magically solve the problem. It won't. You are responsible for deciding whether you can live comfortably in a sexless relationship. If you believe that physical intimacy is too important to compromise, then don't think about marriage until after you and Gary have received competent professional advice and you know more about whether he is motivated and capable of working on the problem.

2

≋

Mending
the Mind,
Body, and Spirit

Introduction

One needn't be a scholar in female psychology to observe that we women learn to wrap our feelings of shame and inadequacy around us like an old familiar blanket. We may be quick to ask "What's wrong with me?" rather than examining the dispiriting and disempowering forces that make us doubt ourselves, that convince us we're not living up to someone's standards or to the great measuring rod in the sky. The amount of time, energy, and money that we waste in our endless and impossible pursuit of perfection is incalculable.

What's wrong with a focus on self-improvement? Nothing, actually. Working on our own self is a far more rewarding venture than trying to change another person who doesn't want to change.

Finding our way in the world does, in fact, demand a large measure of focus on the self. It requires us to look objectively at our own strengths and weaknesses (we all

have both), to observe and change our part in the relationship problems that keep us stuck, and to take responsibility
for living our own life (not someone else's) as well as possible. But working on the self should be a self-loving task,
and cannot be accomplished in an atmosphere of self-
depreciation, self-blame, or perfectionism.

Women are told these days that personal happiness
and self-esteem must come from *within*. We're just supposed to free ourselves from caring about what other people think of us. This modern message is both accurate and
absurd.

Sure enough, positive self-regard does require an
inner clarity about who we are, apart from what others
want, need, and expect us to be. And the less we're caught
in the emotional grip of what others think of us, the better.
But the notion that we can value ourselves—and evaluate
ourselves—entirely apart from how others respond to us is
unrealistic. We are, first and foremost, social beings. If
"who we are" is devalued and discounted by important
people around us, or by the culture we live in, we will have
to struggle even harder to love and value ourselves, to use
and even acknowledge our competence.

A huge body of psychological research documents the
fact that women in this society have far lower self-esteem
than their male counterparts—a natural consequence of
patriarchy. But I've never been entirely convinced that this
is so. I think that feeling inadequate is part of the human
condition, and it just manifests itself differently for each
gender. When a woman feels inadequate, she may eat (or
diet), or shop, or go to therapy, or tell her friends how fat,
ugly, and incompetent she feels, or otherwise wear her vulnerability on her sleeve. When a man feels inadequate, he
may seek emotional distance, or act at the expense of others, asserting his dominance over those who are less powerful than himself. Of course, we all may do some of both.

The reasons for low self-regard or personal unhappiness are difficult to decipher. Women commonly become negatively focused on a particular aspect of the self—fat thighs, a boring personality, minimal accomplishments, no partner, whatever. We may believe that if we could only fix this or that aspect of ourselves, everything else would fall into place. The actual sources of our dissatisfaction and low self-esteem may be obscured from our own view.

Perhaps we're living in a way that compromises our deepest values, beliefs, and desires. Perhaps we do not have clear goals or a life plan. Possibly we're navigating an important relationship in a less than solid way, or not addressing what truly matters to us. Maybe we face discrimination and unfairness on a daily basis. Countless factors from within and without can contribute to our dissatisfaction. Yet our experience might be that everything would be fine if we just became tighter or smaller or lost those ten extra pounds.

Our feeling of emotional well-being will always fluctuate, challenging us most during the stressful times that life inevitably brings. Each person's life includes some hardship and tragedy, if not now, then later. On a smaller scale, disappointment, confusion, and hard times will always be with us. We can expect, at each stage of the life cycle, some assault to the body, mind, heart, and spirit, as life takes a difficult or painful turn.

As the philosopher Ludwig Binswanger sagely put it, "Life is one thing after another." The more centered the self, the more solid our connections to others, the more humor, perspective, and balance in our lives—the better we'll handle whatever surprises life plunks down in our path.

I've Never Had an Orgasm

Dear Harriet:

I am twenty-four years old and I've had two long-term sexual relationships. I've never had an orgasm in my life, despite the fact that both boyfriends tried every technique in the book. Now that I'm single again my friends are urging me to masturbate as a way of finally having an orgasm. I think masturbation is wrong for me, and I don't want to force myself to try it when it makes me so uncomfortable. I wonder if I should just wait until after I'm married to discover my real sexual self? What do you think about masturbation and my dilemma?

Dear Reader:

Your friends obviously care about you and want to be helpful. But you need to listen first to the wisdom of your body, not to your friends, or even to expert advice.

Don't force your body to do anything it doesn't want to do. This includes masturbation, as well as having orgasms. Learn to love your body without pushing it to do what it doesn't want to do, or to feel what it's not feeling.

My own views on masturbation are positive. Our bodies belong to us, or, more accurately, we are our bodies. If we are not entitled to touch ourselves—or to decide not to—who is? Why would we grant another person—even a spouse or lover—a right to our bodies that we don't feel entitled to ourselves?

Masturbation is a normal way to give ourselves pleasure, to relieve tension, and to know ourselves. It offers us the privacy, freedom, and control with which to relax and pay attention to our rhythms, sensations, and desires. This is important since, more often than not, women are taught to pay attention to the passions we arouse in others rather than to our own pleasure.

We come to know and love ourselves, including our bodies, through both solitude and connection. Each enhances but does not substitute for the other. Regretfully, sexuality in relationships is usually encumbered by enormous emotional baggage. Many women have difficulty staying "in the moment" and feeling whatever we are (or are not) feeling. Instead, we may prod our bodies to feel aroused or to achieve orgasm. Our attention may shift to how we look, what our partner is thinking, whether we are taking too long to get excited, to come, or whatever.

> Women are taught to pay attention to the passions we arouse in others rather than to our own pleasure.

Irrespective of sexual orientation, large numbers of women fake orgasm, make exaggerated displays of sexual pleasure, lie or pretend about some aspect of their sexuality, and have sex when they would rather go to sleep. In our culture, sexuality remains one of the most contaminated and compromised aspects of women's lives. Most little girls are not even told that they have a vulva that includes a clitoris. Many are sexually abused or taught body shame, fear, and self-hatred. Masturbation allows us to connect with and pay attention to our bodies' honest messages.

On the subject of female orgasm, you might invite friends to share their experiences, not their advice, although keep in mind that some folks exaggerate their sexual responses in the telling. If you're comfortable doing so, consider speaking to women in your family about how they formulated some of their views on masturbation and sexuality. You might talk with a sister, for example, about the sexual climate in which you were raised.

If you're feeling courageous, you may want to experiment with touch. Try deleting the word *masturbation* from your consciousness. Touch your elbow, cheek, belly, vulva, hair, neck, nipple—without dividing your body or your responses into the categories of "sexual" and "not sexual." You are all you. We all need to free ourselves from the false dichotomous categories we have been raised with: "When I touch myself *here* it is sexual. When I touch myself *there* it is not sexual."

Don't push your body to do or feel anything. The challenge is not to achieve orgasm or to achieve anything but rather to restore connection, self-regard, and self-love.

Should you wait until marriage to try to reach orgasm or to discover your real sexual self? Why defer any quest for self-discovery to the hypothetical future? Marriage can either help or hinder the quest for authenticity and self. On the positive side, we can most fully discover and invent ourselves through relaxed connections with those we love. Yet once we're married it may become extremely difficult for us to distinguish our true feelings from our conditioning, including our wish to keep our man happy—or simply to keep him at all.

Should I Find Out My IQ?

Dear Harriet:

For much of my life, I've worried that I am stupid. I have no learning disabilities, but I have this nagging fear about my intelligence. A friend tells me that she once paid a psychologist to give her an IQ test, and now I am considering doing the same. I feel that if I just knew my IQ, I could stop obsessing about it. But if I learned that I had a low IQ, I'm sure I would be devastated. Do you think I should get tested?

Dear Reader:

As a clinical psychologist who has administered IQ tests for much of my professional career, I can't respond enthusiastically to your idea. Testing is useful in clarifying any number of important diagnostic questions, but not in measuring general intelligence. Moreover, the construction of standardized intelligence tests reflects racial, class, and gender biases. These tests reflect no universal truths about what constitutes intelligence.

An overall intelligence quotient score is also less informative than you might think, because it is arrived at by averaging your individual scores in many different areas. For example, if you achieve very high scores on certain parts of the test and very low scores on others, then your total IQ score might land in the average range. This number would reflect nothing about your special abilities and limitations, even as measured by the test.

Many people secretly fear they're not as smart or competent as other people think they are and that eventually they'll be "found out." Women are especially vulnerable to feeling inadequate, in part because of internalized beliefs promoted by our male-dominated culture about whose work and thinking are important and valuable. When we begin to feel less than equal, we should question these standards and ask, "Who says?"

Who says a man that solves mathematical mysteries is brilliant, when he fails to notice that someone in the room is upset? Who says the ability to grasp the nuances of a social interaction is a lesser measure of intelligence than the ability to grasp the prin- ciples of engineering? I don't mean to imply that some women aren't naturally gifted mathematicians or engineers. My point is rather that traits and abilities typically associated with female experience are not truly valued.

> The richest and most critical aspects of intelligence cannot be assigned a number.

I am continually struck by the remarkable intelligence of women and also by how it is discounted. I hope that you—and all women—will recognize that human intelli- gence comprises more factors than we can ever begin to quantify. Intelligence includes such complex and invalu- able skills as the capacity for friendship, for empathy, for being perceptive, caring, alert, and emotionally present in the world. The richest and most critical aspects of intelli- gence cannot be assigned a number.

I'm So Self-Conscious

Dear Harriet:

I have been shy for most of my twenty-two years. I do fine with people I know, but I have a terrible time when I first meet people in groups. I dislike parties and social gatherings because I feel painfully self-conscious. My two best friends are pushing me to be more spontaneous and outgoing with others, but the pressure only seems to make the problem worse. Any advice?

Dear Reader:

Often in our best efforts to change things, we make them worse. The command to be spontaneous (like the command *not* to think of a purple cow) has a paradoxical effect.

What bothers you about being shy? There are folks who spill out their deepest secrets at office parties, others who are profoundly private, and everything in between. If you could surgically remove your shyness, you might also remove what you most value about yourself. Often, what we like the *very best* and the *very least* about ourselves are one and the same or, more accurately, different variations on the same theme.

> Remember the proverbial centipede that became unable to walk when asked how it moved its one hundred legs.

You would be surprised at how common shyness is and how many people mask it with what seems like standoffishness, social superiority, or feigned confidence. About 48 percent of Americans report that they are shy. Most are able to hide their pounding hearts, churning stomachs, and negative self-evaluations with a calm exterior.

Try to relax and accept yourself. When we watch ourselves we can become like the proverbial centipede that became unable to walk when asked how it moved its one hundred legs. Your best friends are evidence of your capacity for caring and connection. This is far more important than how you fare at cocktail parties and the early stages of relationships.

I'm Not Sure My Therapy Is Working

Dear Harriet:

For a long time now, I haven't felt like therapy is helping me. My therapist says that my desire to quit is one of my problems and has even said that if I leave I will get worse and lose whatever ground I've gained. I very much want to stop therapy, but how do I know if she's right?

Dear Reader:

I don't think it is useful to continue therapy over time if you are spinning your wheels and getting nowhere. Your therapist is your employee; it makes sense to question putting time and money into a service that you are not finding helpful.

Staying in therapy out of fear of stopping is not a solid reason to continue. If you terminate, you can always resume the process at a later date, if need be, and a vacation from therapy may give you the information you're seeking. Nor is it your job to worry about your therapist's feelings. She will survive your leaving her.

That said, the decision to leave therapy is a complicated one because substantive change does occur slowly, and frustrations and derailments are a normal part of the process. And since the therapeutic relationship is often emotionally intense, we can feel compelled to stay or leave for the wrong reasons.

There are countless therapists with different belief systems who work in significantly different ways, so that if one therapist or therapy isn't helping you, another might. Unfortunately, there are few objective and clear-cut guidelines to evaluate the competence of your therapist. The challenge is to think through your concerns as clearly as you can.

It's often not wise to terminate therapy at a time of crisis or turmoil, which is not a time of clear thinking. And consider carefully what your therapist has to say, because she may have a valuable perspective. If you tend to take flight when the going gets rough, that's an important pattern to think about. But keep in mind that it's not a personal failing when you do not find a particular therapist helpful, even if this therapist has helped other people you know.

> Your therapist is your employee. She will survive your leaving her.

Ultimately, you are the best expert on your own self. Seeking feedback from others can be useful, but no one else can—or should—make this decision for you, your therapist included.

Living with Chronic Illness

Dear Harriet:

I am a thirty-year-old French teacher and I have recently been diagnosed with a serious chronic illness. I am receiving excellent medical care, but I'm not coping well with the news. On the one hand, I'm told that having a positive attitude is crucial to my health, yet I'm so depressed and I just can't believe this is happening to me. I feel like my life is over and I don't know where to turn for help.

Dear Reader:

Receiving the diagnosis of a chronic illness can be overwhelming at first. You may wonder about how this illness will affect your relationships, your work, and your plans for the future. It's natural to feel depressed and angry, betrayed by your body, and afraid of burdening others or being abandoned by them.

Knowing your diagnosis is a critical first step in starting to deal with it. You're off to a good start by receiving trustworthy medical care. The next step is to make a personal commitment to come to terms with the emotional aspects of the diagnosis.

You are not alone. Learn as much as you can about how others have coped with the challenge of chronic illness. Support groups are an invaluable

> Friends may advise you to be upbeat because of their own discomfort with your pain.

source of information and camaraderie. Organizations focused on your particular disease can direct you to resources in your own community.

Although it's not useful to drown in despair, it's also not useful to keep a "positive attitude" when this means concealing or denying real emotions. Coming to terms with chronic illness takes persistence and effort, and you wouldn't be human if you could just put your fears out of your head.

For individuals living with chronic illness, dealing with feelings of grief, anger, and fear may be an ongoing task. Flare-ups of the illness or changes in your life situation may lead to new losses and challenges. People around you may advise you to be plucky and upbeat, in part because of their own discomfort with your pain. But remember that your ability to acknowledge that you are depressed and to reach out for help is a strength.

But don't confuse your *initial* response to your diagnosis with how you will cope over the long haul. In time, you will discover your strengths, including your ability to manage hardship and your capacity for optimism, hope, and joy.

I Just Can't Say No!

Dear Harriet:

Here I am in the 1990s, a woman who keeps saying yes when I really mean no. Even when I find the courage to utter that two-letter word, I don't stick to it when my boss, husband, or neighbor gives me a hard time. Do you have any tips for me that will get others to respect my efforts to be assertive, or that will help me not to feel so guilty when I do say no?

Dear Reader:

Women are often far more sensitive to other people's needs than to our own. We are the nurturers, soothers, helpmates, and steadiers of rocked boats. As a result, we may feel guilty if we're anything less than an emotional service station to others.

Changing this age-old pattern is understandably difficult. Other people may react with anger and disapproval. When that happens, it's tempting to step back to

> People won't love you for saying no, so don't expect applause.

our "proper place" and conclude that change is not possible.

Other people's resistance is not the only problem. More important, we haven't established where our responsibility to others ends and our responsibility to ourselves begins. But no one can tell you when it is appropriate to say no, although there's no shortage of advice on the subject. It's your job to decide what's right for you, which may be different from your image of the liberated woman.

People won't love you for saying no, at least not in the short run, so if you become more assertive, don't expect applause. Instead, expect the others person to make a countermove ("How can you be so selfish!") to reinstate the status quo. You can't control such reactions; you can, however, say no in ways that will make people more likely to respect your limits. Here are some suggestions to consider:

1. If you're feeling even slightly uncertain about a request, don't give an immediate answer. No matter how much pressure you feel, you can always say, "I need a little time to think about it. I'll get back to you tomorrow."

2. Choose carefully when you really want to say no. If you don't feel comfortable saying no in a particular situation, that's OK.

3. When you do say no, make sure your explanations are only about you ("I'm not able to take on anything else at this time") and not an implicit criticism of the other person.

4. Don't try to change the other person's response. If your sister is furious that you won't drive her to the airport, don't tell her that she's wrong to feel that way. Instead try, "I understand that you're angry about it, and I'm sorry, but I have so much else going on that day that I think a trip to the airport will be too much."

5. Avoid becoming defensive or providing lengthy explanations for your decision. If you're having trouble being heard, it's fine to say something simple like "I'm not sure why, but I'm just not comfortable doing that."

6. Try to stay calm and low-key, even if the other person reacts strongly. Intensity escalates anxiety.

7. Steer clear of blaming others for your choices and behaviors ("My father is so impossible that I can't say no to him"). Other people may make it hard for you to turn them down, but it's your job to chose how you will respond.

8. Connect with other women in your family (your mother, sister, grandmother, or aunts) to learn how they managed the dilemmas you are struggling with. Have they also had trouble saying no? The more information you have about family patterns, the clearer you will become about your own choices.

9. Go slowly and start small. If you try to change from an accommodating person to an assertive one overnight, you'll rev up a lot of anxiety in yourself and others and end up not changing at all.

10. If you say no in an important relationship, and the other person reacts negatively to your greater assertiveness, try not to distance yourself or retreat into anger.

Changing an old pattern that may have roots in many generations of your family is possible but not easy. You probably will feel guilty. But guilt is not terminal and will eventually subside. And saying no brings with it the possibility of next time saying yes with a lighter heart.

Finally, consider that your difficulty saying no, although admittedly a problem, may also reflect your kindness and generosity of spirit, qualities the world needs more of. Few things are all good or all bad.

I'm Ashamed to Undress
in the Locker Room

Dear Harriet:

I'm ashamed to get undressed in the locker room at the gym. My inner labia hang out like a turkey wattle, and I worry that I look different "down there," although I have no way to know for sure. A friend says I may have been sexually abused as a child, and this is why I'm so uncomfortable with anyone seeing my vagina. What do you think?

Dear Reader:

Be assured that no one but your gynecologist can see your *vagina*. It's your *vulva* that you're worried about—which includes the labia and clitoris. Also be assured that many women experience similar confusion. Our society still hasn't solved the what-shall-we-name-it problem for the

> Few women are unaffected by narrow and unimaginative standards of attractiveness.

female half of the species. Until we can comfortably use the correct words for what we do see "down there," we can't expect women to feel comfortable and familiar with their own bodies.

Women can use a mirror for self-examination but heterosexual females rarely have the opportunity to get accurate visual information (that is, from comparison with other women) that allows us to appreciate of our anatomical variability. As to the "What's normal?" question, vulvas differ widely in style, color, size, and proportion, and many include "turkey wattles."

A woman's shame about her vulva may mask deeper anxieties about sexuality or reflect a history of sexual trauma, but this is by no means always the case. Many women with no history of abuse feel similarly self-conscious. Shame-inducing messages about our bodies and sexuality are everywhere. And few women are unaffected by narrow and unimaginative standards of female attractiveness and acceptability for whatever body part we may happen to focus on.

Am I Codependent?

Dear Harriet:

My friends keep telling me that I am codependent and that I need to join a group to get help with it. I do have a lifelong pattern of taking responsibility for other people's problems and neglecting myself. But I don't like to be called codependent, and I don't know why. Maybe I'm just being defensive. Could you please define the term *codependency.* Is it a mental illness?

Dear Reader:

Codependency is a label of such vast inclusiveness that we are all "it." If you survey the literature, you'll find that codependency is defined as anything that interferes with our capacity for healthy autonomy and intimacy, any underresponsibility for ourselves and overfocus on others, any neglect, sacrifice, or disregard of our own person.

Codependency has been labeled a progressive (albeit treatable) disease by some self-help authors—but most folks use the term more lightly. If women in general are considered codependent, I can assure you it is not because we are sick. Rather, we have learned what our culture teaches—that is, to focus on others at the expense of ourselves.

It makes good sense to resist negative labels of any kind. If your friends have specific complaints about your behavior, ask them to tell you what bothers them without diagnosing you. If they keep trying to fix you, suggest that they form a codependency group of their own.

I'm Afraid I'm a Lesbian

Dear Harriet:

I'm thirty years old and have always thought of myself as heterosexual. A year ago, though, I fell deeply in love with a close woman friend who returns my feelings. Could my attraction to a woman be a reaction to a traumatic relationship with a man which ended eight years ago? I can't see a therapist, because I hold a prominent position in a small town. I am deeply ashamed at the thought of being a lesbian. Why has this happened? What can I do about it?

Dear Reader:

A woman may unexpectedly fall in love with another woman at any stage of the adult life cycle. Some women maintain this same-sex orientation for the rest of their lives and others do not. Your experience is not uncommon, nor is it shameful. What is shameful is the ignorance and prejudice of a society that condemns honest affections.

Why has this happened? If you asked ten different experts, you would most likely receive ten different opinions. We know very little about the nature of erotic passion and what determines our sexual orientation. Falling in love can reflect an irrational, anxiety-driven response or an enduring, solid bond. Time, maturity, and a deep knowledge of our partner ultimately allow us to assess the wisdom of a particular choice, male or female.

What can you *do* about your dilemma? Try to relax and view your struggle as one that will resolve over time. You need not label yourself one way or another, nor must you decide today whom or how you will love next year. Our erotic preferences, our lifestyle preferences, and our emotional preferences, are not always carved in stone.

Try to become less concerned about *what* you are and more comfortable with *where* you are at the present time. Give yourself permission to experience uncertainty, anxiety, and confusion. These are normal feelings that reflect the tension between where your heart has led you and societally induced shame. Eventually, you will experience more clarity.

To this end, don't deal with your problem in isolation. Go to the gay and lesbian section of any large bookstore and begin to educate yourself. Open up conversations with good people who will be sensitive to both your fears and your affections. Connect with gay culture, which is everywhere. Such connections won't make you a homosexual or push you in a false direction. They will simply provide you with more accurate and valuable information. If you're too scared to do this yet, sit still awhile, be patient with yourself, and see where time takes you.

> You need not label yourself one way or another.

Don't shut the door on psychotherapy. Many people starting therapy are afraid that their confidentiality will be violated, or they feel otherwise vulnerable and scared. Consider finding a competent therapist and discuss any concerns up front. Inquire directly about her or his values and beliefs about sexual orientation. Don't hire anyone who believes homosexuality is a sick, unfortunate, or "lesser" choice. You don't need to pay a therapist to increase your shame or narrow your options.

Finally, loving women is *not* the product of a traumatic or failed relationship with a man. If this were so, there would be relatively few heterosexuals roaming the planet.

My Doctor Hugs Me

Dear Harriet:

I see a doctor for monthly appointments related to a skin problem. After each appointment, he gives me a big bear hug, which makes me feel uncomfortable and anxious. I want to confront him about it, but my friends say I'm overreacting, that he's just being friendly. How can I be sure of his intentions? What's the right thing for me to do?

Dear Reader:

You can't be certain of your doctor's intentions. But you do know your own reactions. Respect those feelings, which are signaling to you to protect your personal space. Do this in a way that feels comfortable to you.

You may not need to confront your doctor if you can find a lighter way to avoid or block his hugs, such as reaching out to shake hands when he approaches you. If you are unable to stop his hugging ritual, change doctors. Although his intentions are anybody's guess, his behavior is not appropriate.

> If you can't stop your doctor from hugging you, change doctors.

Help! I'm Too Gorgeous!

Dear Harriet:

Please don't put me down for complaining about this, but my problem is I'm too gorgeous. I have never had close girlfriends, because women feel uncomfortable around me and jealous of my looks. I hate dating because I can't tell whether a man is interested in me solely for my looks, or whether he really wants *me*. I can't tell you how hurtful it is to think that men choose me on the basis of something as superficial as appearance.

Dear Reader:

Your physical presence in the world is not "superficial." True enough, women's sexuality and physical beauty have been badly, even violently, misused. But your beautiful appearance is a gift, and the challenge for you, as for all women, is to love, enjoy, and regard yourself.

Some men will pursue you for your beauty without regarding you as a whole person. But in this you are hardly alone. Countless people, including those of considerable wealth or status, are pursued for the "wrong" reasons. We all face the challenge of evaluating a prospective partner's intentions, values, and character. We all need to use our intelligence, experience, and intuition in deciding whom to trust and love.

Whether you are beautiful or not, relationships are invariably difficult, at least somewhere along the way. Beware of getting overfocused on one problem, your appearance, at the expense of other issues. For instance, can your appearance alone truly account for the absence of female friendship in your life? While some women may initially feel uncomfortable in your presence, that can change over time as you allow yourself to emerge as a real person, with strengths and vulnerabilities. Also, jealousy and competitiveness are as natural among friends as they are among siblings. A solid relationship can endure jealousy just as it can endure anger and the whole gamut of prickly feelings.

Share your experience with other gorgeous women and hear their stories. Also, consider talking openly and

> A woman's beauty—or lack of it—
> tells us virtually nothing about how
> her relationships will fare over the long haul.

frankly about your problem to family members. How do they think your appearance has affected your life—and theirs? Has being gorgeous contributed to your being an insider, or outsider, in your family? Who has overfocused on your beauty, who has ignored it, and who has simply appreciated it? Is the issue of physical appearance a subject that can be addressed calmly and objectively in your family?

Try to enjoy being gorgeous just as someone might enjoy having a dazzling singing voice or remarkable athletic talent. Like many women, you may feel guilty about having more than the usual share of something wonderful, particularly if you perceive others as having a hard time with it.

Also, keep your gorgeousness in perspective. Physical appearance can make a big difference at the start of a relationship. Beyond that, a woman's beauty—or lack of it— tells us virtually nothing about how her relationships will fare over the long haul.

Don't Ask, Don't Tell

Dear Harriet:

My friend Allison invited me to give a lecture about my work as a photojournalist. In introducing me at the event, she was thoughtless enough to reveal my age. I was furious at her insensitivity and at her flagrant violation of my privacy. Allison insists that I'm overreacting. We both want to hear your opinion on the subject. How would you have reacted in my shoes? Is my anger legitimate?

Dear Reader:

Anger is neither right nor wrong, legitimate nor illegitimate. Anger simply is. You have a right to it, just as Allison has a right to her opinions.

If you feel that your privacy has been violated, your anger is particularly understandable. We all seek to exercise control over what we decide to conceal from or reveal to others. We take for granted our right to keep some things to ourselves.

Perhaps you and Allison can both benefit from continuing the conversation. Allison might consider running any future introductions by the speaker in advance. You, along with the rest of womankind, might rethink the shaming messages we learn about growing older—which is, after all, everyone's goal.

As women age, many become more courageous, rebellious, and free-spirited. It is hardly surprising that we are encouraged to remain nonthreatening "girls" rather than to become strong women, and that the wisdom and experience of older women are devalued and ignored.

Consider why we would choose, by concealing our age, to perpetuate the notion that there is anything shameful or lesser in growing older? When we fail to say proudly or, at the very least, matter-of-factly, "I'm forty-two" or "I'm sixty-eight," we participate in a profound act of self-depreciation. We also betray our daughters, who look to us to learn what it means to be an adult woman.

My intention is not to question or criticize what you, *as an individual*, choose to keep private or secret. Rather, I am challenging women, *as a class*, to consider the implications of our mystifying and concealing the number of years we have been alive. The fact that this widespread practice is normalized or culturally sanctioned does not make it less of an assault on our dignity and self-regard. It only makes it harder for us to look squarely at its consequences.

How is the dominant group—that is, men—served by the cultural prescription for women to keep their age a secret, to joke and even lie about it? How are women shamed and disempowered by our complicity with such a world view? It may seem to be a trivial issue, but when women collectively examine the "trivial," the "unimportant," we begin to move toward the center of what keeps us sleepy and subordinate.

I share my age with others much the same way I share the fact that I am a clinical psychologist or a Kansan. The fact that I am fifty-one is an identifying characteristic that allows others to locate me in time and history. Plus, getting older is my primary goal in life, the one on which all my other goals rest.

Occasionally, someone at the podium introduces me with a joke about my age ("Oops! I've almost given away her age up here!"), rather than sharing the fact of it. I'm heartened if nobody in the audience laughs. Whether a joke about my age elicits laughter or not, I myself mention it with pride. Afterward I try, with all due respect for timing and tact, to talk about my reaction with the person who introduced me. If a light-skinned African-American woman was introduced by joking ("Oops! I've almost given away her race!"), we would find the implications unacceptable and not at all amusing.

In your case, your ability to share your reaction with Allison is a strength, as is your forthrightness in telling her what information you consider to be private. I don't agree that you

> I share my age with others much the same way I share the fact that I am a psychologist or a Kansan.

overreacted, because such reactions occur for good reason. It is the culture, not your personal reactions, that I am calling into question. Privacy is a basic, essential human right. In the name of privacy, however, we may preserve lies that oppress us.

I would like to make a bold call to disobedience. I suggest that we share our age with no more apology or reticence than we would feel in sharing, say, our religion or ethnic background. If, together, we stop treating our age like a shameful secret, then the lives of *all* women will be strengthened and enriched.

Can We Cause Our Own Cancer?

Dear Harriet:

My sister, age thirty-four, was recently diagnosed with breast cancer. I do all the right things to prevent and detect this disease: I eat a healthful diet, examine my breasts monthly, and get a yearly mammogram. It worries me, though, when people tell me that cancer is influenced more by personality and psychological factors than by nutrition and genetics. My sister has a tendency toward depression and is rather passive in her daily life, and I'm the same way. We both want to know if this can cause breast cancer.

Dear Reader:

Depression and passivity can be occupational hazards of being raised female—but they do not cause cancer. Your sister is not responsible for creating her disease. She is, however, responsible for living her life as well as possible. All of us die—if not sooner, then later—and nothing positive can be said on behalf of depression and passivity. How we live is more important than how long we live—but living well does not protect us from cancer.

In general, women have become less passive and more self-directed since the second wave of feminism. Yet the rate of breast cancer has doubled since 1961 and has reached epidemic proportions. And although breast cancer is killing women in ever-increasing numbers, research into the cause of breast cancer remains shamefully underfunded. Theories about "cancer-prone personalities" deflect us from using the political process to insist that ade-

quate money be allocated to protect women's lives by finding a cure for this disease.

These theories also obscure the fact that increasing
numbers of young people are victims of environmentally
induced cancers. Those in power who are more concerned
with profits than people would prefer us to maintain a narrow focus on psychological, genetic, and "individual
lifestyle" determinants of cancer. Such a focus deters us
from protesting against the poisoning of our communities
by toxins and carcinogens. Profit madness, not personality
deficit, is the problem.

This reality, however, does not negate the inseparability of mind and body. Research in the field of psychoneu-
roimmunology suggests clear links between our emotional
and physical well-being. When we live joyless, isolated, or
inauthentic lives, our bodies may signal that something is
wrong, in the form of illness or physical distress. When our
relationships are compromised, our immune system may be
compromised as well. Surely our bodies can only be
strengthened when we live examined lives that include a
large share of love, wisdom, courage, and risk.

Yet here are the hard facts. Alarmingly large numbers
of joyful, assertive, and loving women, men, and children
will continue to die prematurely of cancers. Countless
numbers of depressed, passive women will continue to live
into ripe old age. Living right is undoubtedly a good and
healthful idea, but it is no guarantee against getting cancer
or of preventing its return.

Moreover, the diagnosis of cancer does not indicate
that one has not lived well enough, or that one could have

> Any threat to our survival can inspire us to
> be more passionate, clear-eyed, and awake.

prevented cancer by having done (or been) more (or less) of this or that. The fact that we can gather our emotional strength to help heal ourselves does not mean that we are in any way at fault for getting a cancer diagnosis in the first place. This blame-the-victim syndrome is a terrible distortion of our recognition of the healing powers of loving oneself and one's life. Glib prescriptions for cancer patients to "look on the bright side" and "keep a positive outlook" instruct us to clean up our attitude; instead, we more desperately need to insist on clean air, water, and food and a safe livable Earth.

Although your sister's passivity and depression didn't "cause" her cancer, her diagnosis might prompt her to reexamine and change her life. When faced with a threat to survival, we are often capable of taking large and courageous leaps forward. The diagnosis of cancer, like any reminder of our mortality, can awaken us from a psychic slumber and inspire us to be more passionate, clear-eyed, and awake. I hope that you can join your sister in meeting this challenge without having to be motivated by a health crisis of your own.

Is My Fantasy Abnormal?

Dear Harriet:

When I masturbate, I often fantasize that I'm tied down in bed and forced to have intercourse with a group of teenage boys in France. A psychologist friend told me that this "rape fantasy" means I unconsciously want to be raped. I'm incredibly upset by this idea, and I really need help sorting this out.

Dear Reader:

Sexual fantasies are as far-ranging as the human imagination. But any particular sexual fantasy may say nothing about what we actually want in real life.

> What we fantasize about may say nothing about what we actually want in real life.

The nature of a fantasy is that we orchestrate it. When you masturbate, for example, you are 100 percent in charge of the scenario. Imagine, in contrast, how utterly vulnerable and terrified you would feel if you were actually abducted by a group of teenage boys who drove you to a strange house, tied you to a bed, and proceeded to have sex with you.

If you lived to tell the tale, you might later turn this nightmare into an erotic fantasy, in an unconscious attempt to master what happened to you. This does happen to some rape victims. But no woman wants to be raped. Rape is a trauma for all women, no less so for women who fantasize about having forced sex.

Should I Pretend to Be Happy?

Dear Harriet:

I'm continually dissatisfied with my life, and I've been moping around feeling sorry for myself for a long time. My yoga teacher told me that if I smile and pretend to be happy, it will actually help me to feel better. Is this really good advice?

Dear Reader:

It's true that moping around and feeling sorry for yourself—although it may be absolutely necessary at a particular time—can lead to more of the same. Consider your teacher's suggestion as one of many ways you can begin to get a grip on your unhappiness.

Does smiling help? The Buddhist monk Thich Nhat Hanh, a world-renowned spiritual leader and peace activist, encourages us to smile often and notes that the act of smiling relaxes the muscles of the face and has many benefits. His work has inspired many readers to smile as part of a spiritual practice.

But what about pretending? Putting on a happy face is hardly useful if we conceal real feelings that need to be acknowledged, shared, validated, and understood. However, pretending *can* be a bold form of experimentation and inventiveness. Pretending joy or happiness sometimes has the effect of a self-fulfilling prophecy, helping us discover or enhance our capacity for these positive feelings.

However, no amount of smiling can substitute for the hard work of addressing the actual sources of your unhappiness and taking action to solve your problems. And no

> Pretending joy or happiness can be a
> self-fulfilling prophecy.

amount of pretending can substitute for connections to caring people with whom you can be yourself.

Why not experiment with your teacher's suggestion? You'll see whether you ultimately feel more empowered to act on your own behalf—or the opposite.

I Trusted My Doctor

Dear Harriet:

Several months ago I began to have abnormal bleeding and cramping. I believed my gynecologist when he told me I needed an immediate and total hysterectomy. Then a pathology report following my surgery revealed it wasn't necessary after all. I am overwhelmed with rage for allowing him to mutilate my body to make more money for himself. I am also filled with self-hatred for so blindly trusting him. I don't know how to recover from the bitterness I feel.

Dear Reader:

Having an unnecessary hysterectomy is a violation that requires time to cope with. Your feelings of rage—at yourself and your doctor—are normal and predictable. This is not to say, however, that you are to blame or at fault. You did what our culture encourages us to do: you trusted your doctor.

Only relatively recently has attention been focused on the problem of unnecessary hysterectomy (removal of the uterus) and oophorectomy, or ovariectomy (removal of the ovaries). Estimates of the number of hysterectomies thought to be unnecessary range from 10 to 90 percent depending on the source of the study, and they vary according to geographical location.

Individual doctors differ widely in their attitudes toward the surgery. I recently spoke with one physician who *routinely* recommends a hysterectomy for healthy postmenopausal women, on the grounds that their reproductive organs are no longer useful and are a potential site for disease. More enlightened and responsible gynecologists recommend the surgery only when it is absolutely essential to the health of the woman and all other options have been considered.

Don't assume that your doctor operated out of greed. Medicine is an inexact science that leaves much room for differing opinions and wisdom through hindsight. Did your doctor recommend the surgery on the basis of your preoperative pathology report? If so, you can have that report and the slides reviewed by a second pathologist to further assess the validity of his recommendation. If you haven't done so, gather all of the facts and get different perspectives.

> When any kind of surgery is recommended, always get a second (or third) opinion.

Also, give yourself time to grieve your loss, and make every effort to seek support. Any number of activities can help you get a grip on your intense emotions: keep a journal, join a hysterectomy support group, talk with family and friends, become an advocate of women's health issues. Also, explore traditional and natural/alternative approaches you might follow to help alleviate or even eliminate some of the physical and emotional effects of the hormonal depletion you may be experiencing.

If the facts warrant it, you may decide to report your doctor's actions to a medical review board and to make your experience known. You remind us that when any kind of surgery is recommended, we should seek a second (or third) opinion and persist with the help of friends and family, as clear and assertive information seekers.

Should I Quit Group Therapy?

Dear Harriet:

I've been in group therapy for a year. I help others, but I don't feel that I'm getting anything back. The other group members are dealing with major crises in their lives, so they're hardly in a position to offer me constructive feedback on my comparatively stable existence. I really believe my limited time and financial resources could be better invested elsewhere and that it's time to move on. But my therapist insists I'm not ready to go. Should I listen to her?

Dear Reader:

First, ask your therapist why she believes you're not ready to leave the group, and find out what specific changes you need to make for her to give you the green light. Review the reasons why you sought therapy a year ago and what has changed since then. Consider your therapist's perspective along with those of the other group members. Then make your own decision.

Whether you stay or leave, examine what's blocking you from using the group more effectively, that is, *for yourself.* Is there a pattern in your life of giving more than you get, of caring for others at the expense of the self? How good are you, both inside and outside the group, at communicating your own needs and vulnerability—and making yourself heard?

There are several ways to explore this further. First, until you leave the group, consider trying to get the most out of it, and use it as a laboratory to experiment with new behaviors, such as greater openness and self-revelation. Explain that the gravity of other people's struggles makes it harder for you to share (or perhaps even to acknowledge) your own.

At the same time, learn how others view your participation in the group. Do group members feel comfortable

> How good are you at communicating
> your own needs and vulnerability—
> and making yourself heard?

asking you about sensitive issues? Do they tend to see you as having it all together and not needing anything from them? Does anyone else believe that you need to have a serious problem to ask for the group's attention and concern?

Finally, consider what in your family history might program you to silence yourself, to treat your problems as unimportant, or to view others as having little to offer you. Why might you feel reluctant to take center stage?

In the end, you'll be the best expert on whether to stay or leave. Trust yourself. If you continue to feel that the group isn't right for you, name a termination date. While you're still there, however, try to get your time and money's worth out of each remaining session.

My Abortion Haunts Me

Dear Harriet:

Five years ago I had an abortion. I have not been able to forgive myself for murdering my unborn child. Each passing year, I feel worse rather than better. I've become very active in the right-to-life movement, and I do everything possible to stop other women from committing this same crime. Yet I still suffer every day. Several attempts at therapy haven't helped. Must I live with grief and pain forever?

Dear Reader:

As you know from your own experience, your grief will not disappear through your efforts to stop other women from terminating their unwanted pregnancies. To mourn your important loss and move on, you need to focus on *yourself.*

Our beliefs and feelings on abortion are deeply personal. They are shaped by our class, culture, religion, and personal family history, as well as the social and political climate of the day. Our first family is our most influential context. How openly have you discussed your abortion with family members? Who knows and who doesn't know? Who has forgiven you and who has not? Is *forgiveness* valued and practiced in your family? Some families and ethnic groups place a very high value on forgiveness, while others do not. Because guilt and shame flourish in secrecy, consider sharing the emotional pain of your abortion with close family members and other important people in your life.

Most important, learn all you can about the history

of loss and separation in your family. When one individual is stuck in guilt and grief, there are usually other unprocessed losses in the family background that fuel it. Did your parents or grandparents ever deal with an untimely or traumatic loss? If so, did family members support one another and openly share facts and feelings? Who other than yourself has ever drowned in guilt or grief? Who has been blamed, or has blamed themselves, for a death?

> Create a special ritual that will allow you to express your sorrow and grief.

What other losses or difficult separations have you experienced in your life? Your abortion, like a lightning rod, can gather intensity from past losses, including those in previous generations. Whatever is unresolved in one generation will be dealt with more intensely by the next.

You might find it healing to create a special ritual that will allow you to honor the fetus you aborted and express your sorrow and grief. Your ritual can mark the anniversary of your abortion each year and might include a friend or family member who truly understands your anguish.

Consider paying penance for your abortion. This suggestion may seem odd or punitive to those who fail to appreciate the depth of your guilt. If you believe, however, that you have committed murder, you need to make amends. You might, for example, do relief work in a developing country for a year or undertake some other kind of humanitarian action on a local level that involves a major personal sacrifice on your part.

Perhaps your clergy can help you formulate a plan of action that will balance the scales of justice and satisfy your conscience. But please understand you won't be able to make your amends through other women's bodies.

Sugar Pills

Dear Harriet:

Several months ago, my doctor gave me medication for chronic abdominal pain. After the pain went away, he told me he had prescribed a placebo. He says my positive response to these milk-sugar tablets is proof that the pain was in my head and my symptoms weren't real. I feel tricked by his dishonesty and stupid for being so suggestible. I just need to know if this has ever happened to anybody else?

Dear Reader:

The "placebo effect" is a powerful aid for much of what ails us and can relieve a range of very real medical problems, including rheumatoid arthritis, peptic ulcers, postoperative pain, seasickness, and warts. Placebos also have been shown to affect blood-cell count, respiratory rates, and vasomotor functioning.

Placebos can actually alter body chemistry and mobilize the body's capacity to fight disease. This doesn't mean your medical condition was not real or that you are stupid or suggestible. Placebos work precisely because the mind and the body do not inhabit totally separate spheres, and because hope, optimism, and conviction can sometimes help the body restore itself.

As the late Norman Cousins explained, the placebo effect doesn't "fool" the body but rather transforms the will to heal into tangible physical reality. In his words, "The placebo is the doctor who resides within." We know from biofeedback training, creative imaging, meditation, and other self-regulatory practices that, even without placebos, the mind's power can be harnessed to influence the body.

Your relationship with your doctor is a different matter. If you think he violated your trust, then tell him, and if you don't want him to prescribe placebos in the future, let him know that as well. If you believe he trivializes your pain or puts you down, consider changing doctors. Without a mutually respectful relationship between doctor and patient, the healing process will always be compromised.

> Placebos work because the mind and the body do not inhabit totally separate spheres.

3
≈

Friendship Matters

Introduction

A greeting card depicts a young woman telling her female friend, "I'll always be there for you." Inside the card is the postscript, "Unless, of course, I have a date."

The message takes me back three decades to my college days when my friends and I put more real energy into our discussions about men than into all other subjects combined. But even back then, the stereotype didn't hold water. Schmoozing with my friends is what sustained and nourished me, as it does now. I can't recall a time when I considered my friends something to do until a man came along.

True enough, our commitment and capacity for friendship waxes and wanes. We may slight friendships during that early "Velcro stage" of a romantic relationship. We may neglect friends when family or work consume our time and energy. We need friends less—or need fewer friends—at certain points in our lives. Or we may have the least energy for friends when we most need them. But women know that friendships matter deeply.

Friendship is not without its wrenching moments. When I was sixteen my best friend dropped me for another girl because I wasn't "deep" enough for her. I felt devastated, my confidence crushed. A boy might reject me because I wasn't cool enough, or pretty enough, or "his type." But this girl was my soul mate. When she dropped me for another best friend (whom I imagined to be far more complex and interesting than I was), the injury and loss were immense.

What a relief to be grown up, to no longer take rejection so personally, and, more to the point, to have best friends instead of one best friend. I treasure my friends, I count on them, I love them unabashedly, and I call them terms of endearment like "sweetums" and "honey-bunny." Sometimes I get judgmental. But more often I am simply amazed by who they are, their limitations and vulnerabilities only adding to my appreciation of their uniqueness. I resonate with the words of Anaïs Nin, "Each friend represents a world in us."

I'm incredibly grateful for my long-distance feminist network of friends and colleagues, who saved my life, professionally speaking, during an early low point in my career. They energized and supported me when I was most down, and taught me a new meaning of intellectual community and camaraderie among women. I count on my friends to support me through the inevitable low points of authorhood and to provide champagne or hand-holding at the appropriate moments.

Today, I picture concentric circles of women friends in my life, some more peripheral than others, but all of whom count. These circles are stable, but not static. A friend moves away, a new neighbor becomes a friend. A close friend distances, a distant friend seeks greater closeness. Some friends are forever, and no two friendships are the same. Molly Haskell writes of the different forms a friendship can take: "It can run like a river, quietly and sustainingly through life;

it can be an intermittent, sometime thing; or it can explode like a meteor, altering the atmosphere so that nothing ever feels or looks the same again."

I think friendship brings out the best in us, perhaps because the role of friend is freer of false expectations, compromise, and patriarchal rules than any other. A colleague notes that friendship is "formless" and lacks ritual, but herein also lies its strength, its relative freedom from deceit.

It doesn't surprise me that I receive less unhappy correspondence about friendship than about any other category of relationship. Friendship rarely becomes a nest of extreme pathology. I've yet to receive a letter that says: "Dear Harriet: A close friend insults and degrades me, and sometimes hits me. I love her and I don't know what to do." If a friend behaves terribly or evokes awful feelings, we don't just dream of escape—we get out.

Friendship doesn't always come easily or go well. My friend Ellen reminds me that when a colleague presented a passionate talk on women's friendships at a Menninger Women's Conference, a common reaction of the participants was to feel inadequate, to wonder if their friendships measured up to the ones the speaker described. Some women said they didn't have friends, or didn't know how to make them. Probably everyone has felt hurt or deeply disappointed by a friend at some time, or dismayed to recognize mean-spirited feelings of one's own.

But friendship, generally speaking, is what women do best. Novelist Alice Adams puts it most succinctly: "I think women know how to be friends. That's what saves our lives."

Am I Too Needy?

Dear Harriet:

I am twenty-nine years old and have one best friend, Sandy. I don't feel a need for other friends. The problem is Sandy has many "best friends" and doesn't spend as much time with me as I want to spend with her. As a result, she thinks I'm too needy, and I think she isn't available enough. I'm in a lot of pain over it, I have to say. Am I at fault? Do you have a best friend?

Dear Reader:

You are not at fault to want only one friend, or none, for that matter—if such an arrangement works for you. But your pain is evidence that there is a problem. The problem is not that you're "too needy," but rather that you're looking to one person to meet all your needs and she's not accepting the job.

Can you experiment with giving Sandy more space? Try to respect her need to have more than one friendship. If you continue to pursue her, or if you make her too important in your life, she may increasingly avoid you.

> When we depend on one friend to meet all of our needs, that person can't help but disappoint us.

Like Sandy, I have a number of "best friends" as well as friends I see less frequently who are also important to me. Each friend contributes something unique in the way of wisdom, support, and just plain good times. Having a community of friends helps me not to overreact to the limitations of any one friend.

Author Carolyn Heilbrun wrote these words: "Friendship demands intimacy without ritual . . . love without patterns of loving. It does not require the expression of desire where desire is not felt—nor will it survive the withholding of genuine response. Because it is not institutionalized, friendship is safe from the hazards of daily routines, which, pretending to promote intimacy, defeat it."

When we depend on one friend to meet all of our needs, that person can't help but disappoint us. And the more we seek exclusivity in friendship, the more it becomes obligatory and the less likely it is to fulfill the wonderful vision of what true friendship can be.

My Friend Is Dating a Jerk

Dear Harriet:

My close friend, Nydia, is involved with a man, Ray, who exploits her—just like her last boyfriend did. He keeps borrowing money from her and never pays it back. Nydia bails him out, but then complains to me that she's broke. What do I say to her? I feel a duty to warn her that Ray is bad news, but she gets furious whenever I criticize her boyfriends. To save our friendship, I say nothing. But I hate this jerk, so that doesn't feel right either.

Dear Reader:

I appreciate your dilemma, but if you're locked into a position of silence, your relationship with Nydia will become increasingly distant. Both honor and intimacy are sacrificed in friendship when we can't find a way to talk about things that matter. And Nydia will sense your disapproval whether or not you remain silent.

Of course, you also know from experience that criticizing Ray, or trying to convince Nydia to leave him, won't help. It usually doesn't. When we try to convince another person of "the truth" or assume an I-know-what's-best-for-you attitude, that person will have less emotional space in which to gather the motivation, competence, and courage to solve—or even see—her own problem.

Moreover, we can't really know what another person needs to do at a particular point in time. It's difficult enough to know this for ourselves. No one can fully understand why Nydia chooses men who exploit her, or how this pattern serves or protects her, and when, if ever, she will be ready to change it.

Can you get to a place in your heart where you can honestly put aside your need for Nydia to leave Ray right now or to see him the same way you do? The less you need a particular response from her, the more creative you can be in sharing some of your observations and concerns. For example, you might comment on the *pattern* you observe without blaming Ray or telling Nydia what to do. You might say, "Nydia, I understand your worry about money. As I see it, you're very good at *giving*—and the guys you choose are very good at *taking*. When I think back to your last boyfriend, I hardly ever remember your saying no to him."

Try to let go of wanting your friend
to be who she's not.

Stay focused on Nydia's part of the problem, the only part she can change. Nydia's struggle is one that many women will relate to—she may not truly value and regard herself; she has difficulty clarifying the limits of what she can do or give; she doesn't expect much from men; she compromises too much of herself in relationships.

Sure, you might wish Nydia could say to Ray, "If you don't pay back what you owe me, I'm out of here," but try to let go of wanting her to be who she's not. If you can lighten up and shift into a more neutral gear, you'll feel less frustrated. You'll be able to speak more openly to Nydia, not because you expect anything from her, but because you love her and want to be real with her.

Lending Money to a Friend

≋

Dear Harriet:

An old friend wants to borrow $5,000 from me to enable her to move. I have the money, but I have mixed feelings about going ahead with the loan. I'd feel better if something were in writing, but I'm not sure what to put on paper, and I don't want her to think I don't trust her. What is your philosophy about lending money to friends?

Dear Reader:

It's always hard to say no to a friend in need of money when you are able to make a loan. I don't have a personal philosophy about lending friends money. Instead, I decide on a case-by-case basis when it comes up, which isn't often.

If you're serious about lending money to this friend, put all your concerns and expectations on the table. What if something unforeseen happens and she can't pay you back on time? How might this complication affect your friendship? How do you expect to be repaid? (I have found that it's best to negotiate small regular payments rather than big lump sums.) If you are charging interest, how will it be figured? Do you want payment to continue in the unlikely event that one of you dies before the balance is paid off?

Putting everything down on paper does not communicate a lack of faith but instead makes good business sense. A written agreement saying how much she owes you and when and how the sum will be paid back, signed by both parties, will provide both of you with a clear understanding of the expectations. If your friend has to come back to you

> A written agreement doesn't communicate
> a lack of faith. It protects your friendship
> against future misunderstandings.

later to renegotiate payment, a written agreement will make the process clearer and easier for both of you. Rather than jeopardize the friendship it can help preserve it by ensuring against misunderstandings.

Here's what a note might look like, signed by both parties. The note can be notarized.

INSTALLMENT NOTE AND PAYMENT TERMS

Principal:	$5,000
Interest:	None
Date:	September 20, 1995
Term of Note:	5 years
Quarterly Installment:	$250
Payments due:	December 20, March 20, June 20, September 20

Sue Wolin promises to pay Joan Padilla the sum of $5,000. This sum represents an interest-free loan from Joan Padilla. Sue Wolin promises to pay $250 in equal quarterly installments beginning December 20, 1995, and continuing for five years. This debt shall not terminate upon the death of Sue Wolin or Joan Padilla.

I,_____ , and _____ agree to the terms of this note.

Money is an emotionally loaded subject that causes more misunderstandings between friends and family members than almost anything else. If you value your friendship, it's wise, not selfish, to be extra careful. As Cyndi Lauper says in her hit song, "Money changes everything."

A Friend in a Wheelchair

Dear Harriet:

I just got back from shopping in a computer store with my friend, Katie, who is in a wheelchair. Katie asked all the questions, because she's a computer expert. But the store clerk directed his answers only to me and refused to look at her. This happens all the time, and I'm not sure whom it upsets more—her or me. Why do people act this way? What can I do to fix the problem?

Dear Reader:

It sounds as if the store clerk feels uncomfortable or anxious dealing with a woman in a wheelchair. People fear all kinds of physical differences, and especially those that remind us of our own vulnerability. We relax when we get to know the "different other" as a real person. The clerk may just need more experience—and a push to behave appropriately.

The next time something like this happens, look at Katie instead of at the store clerk if he directs his answers to you. Don't shift your gaze away from her face while the clerk speaks. Meanwhile, Katie should look the clerk in the eye. This consciousness-raising technique can be effective, whether the two of you are in a computer store or at a cocktail party.

But don't do anything if you're acting on Katie's behalf (rather than your own) and you haven't talked to her first about the problem. She may not want your help dealing with this guy, or she may have her own ideas about how to handle him.

I'm Jealous of Her Success

Dear Harriet:

I'm a commercial artist. So is my best friend, Beth, whom I've known since college. For five years we've both enjoyed a moderate level of success, but suddenly Beth is getting a lot of money and recognition for her paintings. Her work is fabulous and I admire her talent. But the problem is I feel envious. I find myself wishing that so much wouldn't come her way. Is it normal to feel so competitive with a close friend?

Dear Reader:

Of course your feelings are normal, and it's a strength that you can recognize them. Friendships suffer not from competition but rather from the denial of it.

Many women learn to dread competition. But when you don't acknowledge an "unacceptable" feeling, such as your envy of Beth, you run the risk of acting it out by ignoring or devaluing her work. Fortunately, you can appreciate Beth's talent even though her success is hard for you.

Many factors contribute to the intensity of the envy we feel toward friends, including our place in our first family and our access to resources and rewards in our current work system. The history of a friendship is also important. Had Beth been an acclaimed artist when you first became friends, you might not be having difficulty with her current success. Starting at the same level heightens competitive feelings when one person then moves forward faster than the other.

Accept your feelings and try to focus on your own work. And keep in mind that our friendships with women are invaluable; they can survive anger, envy, competition, and the entire range of emotions that make us human.

> Our friendships suffer not from competition but from the denial of it.

My Friend Isn't There for Me When I'm Down

Dear Harriet:

My friend Jamie has a hard time when I'm down or depressed. She wants me to just "get over it." If I don't quickly cheer up, she disappears or acts irritated. When I confront her, she admits it's true, but doesn't change. We've been friends for over a decade, and I can't understand how she can have so little heart. Why does she distance from me when I need her the most?

Dear Reader:

Jamie's aversion to depression is probably an anxiety-driven response, not a defect of the heart. Her behavior doesn't necessarily signify a lack of caring, but may simply be her way of getting comfortable when she's feeling anxious.

Distancing is a common way that human beings manage emotional intensity in relationships—which is not to say that it's the mature or responsible thing to do. Jamie's friendship, even with its serious limitation, can still enrich your life, but you need other close friends who have the capacity to be there for you when you're having a hard time.

How can we understand Jamie's behavior? She may feel at a loss about how to be helpful. She may be scared of identifying and acknowledging her own depression, even to herself. Or it may be that when she was growing up,

Jamie's parents over- or underreacted to her expressions of pain and sadness.

> Distancing is a common way that human beings handle emotional intensity in relationships.

Our first family is our most influential context in shaping how comfortable and "present" we can be with another person's emotional pain—and with our own. Have you asked Jamie how feelings of vulnerability and sorrow were shared in her family, and how others responded to her own painful feelings?

If you approach Jamie without judgment and without the expectation of change, you may gain some perspective on why she puts on her track shoes whenever you feel down. Most important, until things with Jamie change, turn elsewhere when you need reliable and consistent support from a friend.

Angry with Fat Friend

Dear Harriet:

My best friend, Lois, is fat. She dresses with style, but she eats huge quantities of fast food and never watches her diet. I'm angry and frustrated by her self-destructive eating, which is due to her low self-esteem. I've done everything conceivable to motivate her to change. I've even offered her ten dollars for every pound she loses. Please help me help her!

Dear Reader:

The most helpful strategy is to stop trying to be so helpful. Focusing on Lois's weight, and trying to "fix" her, will only make matters worse. If you're so intense about her eating habits, she'll have less emotional room in which to struggle with them herself. You know from experience that your attempts to shape her up (or down, in this case) go nowhere.

Try to dim your worried focus on Lois and instead turn the spotlight where it belongs—on yourself. What are your own issues about food and fat? Do you often take an I-know-what's-best-for-you attitude with others? What problems in your own life might you be avoiding by focusing so intensely on Lois?

> It's always advisable to become less of an expert on others and more of an expert on oneself.

It's always advisable to become less of an expert on others and more of an expert on oneself. We inspire our friends through the example of our lives, not through lecturing, admonishing, bribing, criticizing, or psychoanalyzing.

Tell Lois that you worry about her eating habits because you care for her and want her to be as healthy as possible. But hold your tongue until you can share your reactions without judgment and without needing her to eat the way you do or look the way you want her to.

She Always Betrays My Confidence

Dear Harriet:

Mary, my friend of five years, can't keep her mouth shut. Recently I told her something about my husband's family and swore her to secrecy. Within days she had told another friend. This happens all the time. I have talked to her about this problem over and over. She apologizes profusely, then does it again. Why does she do this? What can I do about it?

Dear Reader:

We can never know for sure *why* other people behave as they do. To know this about ourselves is difficult enough. A more useful question is why you continue to confide in someone who, for whatever reason, is unable to honor your confidences.

You can't change Mary (you've already tried), although she may mature in time. Instead, find other friends to confide in, and accept Mary's limitation. Yes, it's a big one in your relationship with her. But with five years of friendship behind you, perhaps you can love her anyway.

> The real question is why you continue to confide in someone who is unable to honor your confidences.

I'm the Only One Who Can Help

Dear Harriet:

My good friend Jan is dying from a progressive illness. Every day after I leave my job as a nurse, I go to care for her in her home and cook her dinner before returning to my apartment. I'm the only person Jan really wants around her, but she's very demanding and I'm feeling overwhelmed and exhausted. Some days I feel so desperate that I think I'm having a mental breakdown. When I suggest to Jan that she find other people to help her, she says she can't, she wants only me. Please help.

Dear Reader:

Whether we're dealing with an aging parent, a sibling, or a close friend, we all struggle to sort out where our responsibility to others ends and our responsibility to self begins. It's easy to blame the other person for being "too demanding," but it's ultimately our responsibility to clarify what we can and cannot do.

Jan may prefer to have only you helping her, but she needs a team of people. You can still do a lot for her, while scaling back on how much you currently handle. You've absorbed as much stress as a person can tolerate, and you need now to give voice to your own vulnerability. This means saying to Jan and to others, "There are limits to what I can do."

You might say, for example: "Jan, we are in a place where we both could use more support. Acknowledging this is painful for both of us. I know it's painful for you because of what you're going through, and for me because

I'm watching you go through it and I love you. We need to get other people involved, because I can't do it all by myself."

> We all struggle to sort out where our responsibility to others ends and our responsibility to self begins.

Let friends and family (both yours and Jan's) know that you're feeling physically exhausted and totally depleted. Be prepared to repeat this message over and over. If Jan responds by becoming emotional and upset, which she may very well do, try to listen to her with an open heart, but don't back down or get defensive or critical.

You can be a loving friend and still set clear limits on what you can do. If you continue to be the only person who is really in charge—without involving other people in Jan's care and without getting support for yourself—the situation will only worsen and you won't be of any help to her, yourself, or anyone else. A mental breakdown will provide you with a guilt-free ticket out of your caretaking role. But this "solution" comes with such a high price tag that I don't recommend it.

My Best Friend Is Jealous

Dear Harriet:

My best friend, Glenna, has kept her distance from me for some time, and I suspect she may be jealous. I've had a bunch of real successes lately (new job, new man), and she has had a bunch of failures. I love her a lot and I wonder whether I should ignore the distance to give her more time to get over it, or confront her in an honest way.

Dear Reader:

Since this is an important friendship and the distance has persisted, it makes sense to find a way to address it. You might begin by moving toward Glenna: make more contact and spend more time together. Between your new job and new boyfriend, Glenna may be thinking that *you* are the one who wants or needs more distance.

If this doesn't help, comment on the distance directly and ask Glenna for her perspective: "Glenna, it seems like you've had less time for me over the past few months, and when we're together there seems to be more tension. What do you think is going on?"

Share your feelings in a nonblaming way. For example: "Glenna, I feel that things have been more distant between us since the fall, which was the time that I got my

---

> Between your new job and new boyfriend,
> your friend may think that you are the one
> who wants distance.

new job and started dating Bob. One of my fears about going through such big changes is that the people I love might back off from me. Maybe that has more to do with my own fears about success. But I wanted to ask you what sort of reactions you've been having to all this and how you think it might be affecting our friendship."

Avoid diagnosing Glenna ("I think you're envious"). Instead, share your own feelings, positive and negative, about the changes in your life. You may even find that you and Glenna have different ideas about what constitutes success and failure in your respective lives.

Starting a Women's Group

Dear Harriet:

Several months ago I started a women's group with five other women from my community. We meet one evening a week at my house with an open agenda. Unfortunately, there are some kinks. One woman refuses to reveal herself despite pressure from the rest of us to open up. Another complains that she feels uncomfortable being the only African-American in the group. Of the six of us, four want the group to focus on individual problems while two want us to deal only with larger women's issues on a less personal level. Is it hopeless?

Dear Reader:

It's invaluable for women to get together on a regular basis to share their personal experiences, and you deserve praise for taking the initiative and starting a group. Modern feminism began with the consciousness-raising group—a powerful source of support, learning, and transformation. In contrast to therapy, women's groups are free, and anyone can start one.

Making a group work, however, is not easy, because of individual differences. While each of us might feel most comfortable huddling in a circle with women who are just like us, this is not challenging or even possible.

Your group will offer the greatest opportunity for the growth of its members if room is made to tolerate or, better yet, appreciate one another's individuality. Try not to judge, but to listen and understand.

Some of us are comfortable sharing our most personal information with relative strangers. Others are private and do not easily self-disclose. Some of us come out of family or ethnic traditions that place a high value on aggressively confronting whatever is considered unjust or wrong. Others are taught that hearts and minds are changed by patience, love, and endurance. Such differences are not a matter of right or wrong, better or worse.

If your group is successful, over time it should become a safe place where people can be themselves. What bothers you about a quiet group member? Granted, it may be helpful to inquire about her silence and clarify whether something about the group blocks her participation. It is equally important, however, to respect her style and her ability to decide how she wants to use the group.

> In contrast to therapy, women's groups are free, and anyone can start one.

What about the discomfort of your one African-American member? Here, the problem is tokenism; that is, the dilemma of numerically scarce individuals in group life. When minority group members exist only in token numbers in a group, they are constrained from behaving naturally whether or not they know it.

Tokens may be numerically scarce females in a male-dominated work group, or one woman of color in an otherwise white women's group. Research suggests that the negative impact of tokenism reflects relative numbers, not people's bad intentions. So, if you are committed to your African-American member, encourage her to invite at least two more women of color into the group.

If you begin to balance your numbers, you can be sure that the subject of racism will emerge, and members become more honest when their numbers are reinforced. The group process may feel anxious for a while, but if you go this difficult route, all group members will ultimately be enriched by the process.

Here are a few other suggestions to help your group along:

Rotate the location of the group so that each member who is willing and able hosts a meeting at her home. If you continue to meet only at your place, the other members may begin to feel as if it's *your* group.

Try to reach a consensus about the ground rules. For example, when I joined a women's group that lasted almost two decades, we had these few rules: the group started at 8:30 P.M. every Wednesday and we aimed to end by 10:30 P.M.; members were expected to call if they couldn't come or would be late; discussions were kept confidential; people could talk about whatever mattered to them.

Of course, reaching a consensus is not easy in the face of differences. The best way to proceed is for each woman to clarify the "I" ("I would like to be able to bring my problems to the group and get people's reactions"). When members speak only for themselves, it allows individual preferences to emerge and helps the group to make better decisions, based on compromise and negotiation.

The challenges you face exist in all of group life. How do we enhance ourselves without diminishing another? How do we celebrate differences rather than suppressing them? How do we create a women's group—and a world—in which none of us has to leave a part of herself at home? How can our wish to understand the other person become as great as our wish to be understood?

These are large challenges. A women's group is a good place to start working on them.

Have I Sold Out?

Dear Harriet:

I recently took a job modeling in the nude for a wealthy professional artist. The job is totally safe, and I make thirty dollars an hour, which is fabulous pay for me. The problem is my best friend, Chloe, says I've sold out. I landed the job because I'm considered beautiful, and she says I have compromised my feminist values for money. I do feel like a hypocrite because I once criticized another friend for modeling. And while I need the money and I truly like the work, I can't stand Chloe's criticism and her insistence that she'd never want this job. I'm tempted to quit. Am I really a sellout?

Dear Reader:

None of us can say with certainty what we wouldn't do until we have the opportunity to turn down the chance. Chloe is convinced she wouldn't take your job for any amount of money. This may or may not be true. There was a time when you, too, were critical of someone who modeled nude.

More important, Chloe's choices say nothing about what's right or best for you. You and Chloe are two different people, so it makes sense that you don't have identical values, priorities, or wants. You have a right to your choices, and Chloe has a right to her reactions.

In friendship, as in other close relationships, we are all vulnerable to feeling envious, which may be expressed indirectly through disapproval. Or we may get anxious when a friend expresses her differences, takes an unpredictable turn, or fails to see things our way. Chloe may be struggling with any or all of the above, or with any number of personal issues that can fuel such a negative response.

Perhaps you could ask her more about her reactions, without getting defensive or critical in return. What aspect of the modeling does she believe compromises your values? How angry is she at you for seeing it differently? If you're

> None of us can say with certainty what we wouldn't do until we have the opportunity to turn it down.

feeling hurt and rejected, let Chloe know that her disapproval is hard on you and that you value her friendship.

When we are true to our own selves, we may risk incurring other people's criticism. But sacrificing your job to preserve the peace with Chloe isn't a terrific idea. Close friendships can usually survive periods of anger and distance. But if the only way to keep a friend is to see things her way, or betray your genuine desires, then the friendship doesn't have a chance.

To Lift or Not to Lift

Dear Harriet:

At the age of forty-seven, my best friend is having a face-lift. She really doesn't need it. I feel so angry with her that I am refusing to drive her to her surgery, which she asked me to do. I just can't support her choice in any way. What is your reaction to plastic surgery and to my situation in particular?

Dear Reader:

If a good friend decided to have a face-lift, I would hope not to judge her. I'd be frank with her about my opinions and I'd encourage her to gather information and think her decision through as carefully as possible. But in the end, yes, I'd drive her to surgery, hold her hand, and be happy for her if she was pleased with the results.

I personally believe it's both possible and natural to love and honor our bodies (our face included), no matter how old, saggy, or "different" looking we may be. But women are encouraged to feel unhappy, even desperate, about the natural aging process, and to experience shame and disconnection from our place in the life cycle. We're bombarded with messages that we're not OK the way we are.

You may wish that your friend would not succumb to these dispiriting forces or submit to the surgeon's knife. But friendship requires a profound respect for differences. If you stay angry, it's unlikely that either of you will understand the other or feel truly understood.

She Said/She Said

Dear Harriet:

I have two close friends, Jo and Brittany. The three of us have been inseparable for a year. Recently Jo stopped speaking to Brittany because Brittany betrayed her confidence. What Brittany did was terrible, but I don't want to drop her. Jo wants me to stop being friends with Brittany, and I want Jo to forgive Brittany. Now Jo and I are fighting. What advice can you offer?

Dear Reader:

Try to remain friends with each of them, and stay out of the conflict between them. Don't push Jo to forgive Brittany, and don't try to patch things up between them. It's unlikely to help.

Staying out of the middle doesn't mean keeping silent about what you believe. If Jo says, "How can you still be friends with Brittany after what she did to me?" share an honest response. For example, "Jo, I don't approve of what Brittany did and I've told her that. I certainly understand that it's too painful for you to be friends with her right now. But it's just not my way to cut off from a close friend because I'm mad at her. I hope you can accept this, because I love you and I don't want to lose our friendship."

> Staying out of the middle doesn't mean keeping silent about what you believe.

You can tell Jo that you can't help but hope that she and Brittany will work things out together over time because you care about them both. But understand that Jo may or may not forgive Brittany (and you) down the road. What's most important is that you navigate each relationship in a way that reflects your values and feels solid to you.

Can't Take a Compliment

Dear Harriet:

I know an incredible woman, Mia, who can't take a compliment. When someone tells her she has done a brilliant or extraordinary job, she says, "It's nothing"—or even grimaces. Why does sincere praise bother some people?

Dear Reader:

Perhaps Mia thinks the praise is inflated. If so, she may feel uncomfortable or even fraudulent receiving it. Mia might accept compliments with more ease and grace if people dropped the superlatives (for instance, try "Great job," rather than "Brilliant job"). Many women don't appreciate their full value and worth, or even if they do, they may not want to be elevated too high above others. It's a matter of opinion whether this is a virtue or a weakness.

A woman's response to being singled out as "special" is shaped by her experience in her first family. Every family, and every ethnic group, has a tradition that has evolved over many generations about whether it's OK for an individual to dazzle or shine. In some families, children are encouraged to take center stage and to boast about getting an A or hitting the winning home run. In other families, the unspoken rule is that children—and adults—perform quietly and without fuss.

Our role in our first family can program us to have a hard time with praise. This is particularly so if our "specialness" occurred at the expense of another family member who was undervalued. (For example, Dad treats little

Annie like a star but treats his wife as if she's dull.) It's difficult to accept and evaluate praise objectively if we were overvalued in our first family. And it's difficult to believe praise if we were undervalued, if our strengths and talents went unrecognized.

Women in particular have difficulty owning up to superlatives. Modesty is still considered the hallmark of successful femininity. Even intellectually liberated women may unconsciously feel frightened and guilty about "hurting" others, or incurring their envy, when they are singled out for accolades and praise.

> Modesty is still considered the hallmark of successful femininity.

If Mia is a good friend, you can ask her to tell you how she perceives other people's compliments and her own response to them. It's an interesting subject to discuss, because no one is immune to having mixed feelings about flattery and praise. We may take praise too seriously and have an inflated sense of our own worth. Or we may be *so* humble that humility becomes its own form of arrogance.

What's Wrong with Giving Advice?

Dear Harriet:

Why has advice-giving suddenly gotten such a bad rap? I always give advice to friends with problems because I have useful ideas to offer. Now I'm told that I'm codependent and that I should not try to fix my friend's problems. People have been fixing one another's problems since the beginning of time. Don't *you* give advice? What are friends for?

Dear Reader:

Sure, I give advice. I even get paid for doing so. Advice-giving plays a valuable role in my friendships as well. There is nothing "codependent" about offering or receiving advice.

But there is advice-giving—and then there is advice-giving! So, what's *not* helpful?

It's not helpful to give advice to a person who doesn't want it—who just wants you to listen and be present for her. Advice-giving is also of dubious value to people who say they want your advice but consistently fail to heed it.

Advice is rarely helpful when we deliver it in an intense, I-know-what's-best-for-you way. It's fine to give advice if we recognize that we are only sharing an opinion ("In my experience, this has worked for me . . ." or "I see it this way . . ."). However, if we feel angry or frustrated because the other person doesn't follow our advice, it's a good indication that we shouldn't be giving it.

Moreover, advice can kick relationships out of balance if we are better at giving it than receiving it. If we consider it our sacred calling to fix others, we may do less well at sharing our own vulnerability and seeing others as having something to offer in return.

In some friendships and circumstances, the most helpful thing we can do is *not* to be helpful. Rushing in to offer advice—like rushing in to cheer someone up—may reflect our own inability to remain emotionally present in the face of another person's problems and pain. If we move in too quickly with solutions, we can make it harder for others to be in touch with their own competence and inner resources. Learning to be a caring listener and a skilled questioner can go a long way toward empowering others to find their own solutions.

Why not ask your friends for feedback about your style? Do they think you come across like a know-it-all—or that you're trying to shape them up to think the way you do? Do they feel you don't respect their ideas when they differ from yours—or that you don't listen well enough?

> If we feel angry when the other person doesn't follow our advice, it's a good indication that we shouldn't be giving it.

If you talk to your friends, you may discover it's the *way* you give advice that's getting in the way. You have nothing to lose by approaching your friends and soliciting *their* advice about your advice-giving.

How Can I Win My Friends Back?

≋

Dear Harriet:

I've just ended a two-year passionate romance. During this time, I totally dropped all of my friends. They're mad and I feel like a dog. How can I heal my friendships and get back on my friends' good sides?

Dear Reader:

You can offer each friend a heartfelt apology, along with your perspective on what happened ("When I fall in love, I tend to lose myself in the relationship. I know I've neglected you and I'm terribly sorry"). But don't expect an immediately positive response, and don't pressure friends to take you back into their intimate lives before they're ready. Two years of cutoff is a long time. The process of reconnecting may be slow and bumpy.

Steamy starts are compelling, but when we isolate ourselves in relationships, we put more than our friendships at risk. We also lose our capacity to look clearly and objectively at our partner, ourselves, and the romantic encounter. And we may have nothing—not even our self-respect—to return to when the relationship ends. Consider what steps you can take to avoid a repeat performance.

> When we isolate ourselves in a steamy relationship, we may not have our friends— or our self-respect—to return to when the relationship ends.

4

Women
at Work

Introduction

When I was growing up, a career was considered something to fall back on for the unlucky gal whose husband died or left her, or for those who couldn't find a husband at all. The rules of the game were clear and simple. Men were supposed to *be* somebody. Women were supposed to *find* somebody.

Inside my Jewish home, however, the highest emphasis was placed on education and achievement. As far back as I can remember, my father talked about "my two daughters, the doctors," to anyone who would listen. As small children, my sister, Susan, and I knew we would each obtain a doctorate the way other girls knew that they would graduate from high school.

I'm grateful that my family's values pushed me forward, because the cultural message of the day ("A woman must be smart enough to get a man but never to outsmart him") did not. Even as a young adult, I was given dispiriting mixed messages about success, like when a renowned

New York psychiatrist diagnosed me as having penis envy. He was convinced that my intellectual and competitive strivings reflected an unconscious attempt to compensate for my lack of the coveted male organ. Like many experts of the day, he thought it regrettable that certain woman had to resolve their neurotic conflicts by getting out of the house.

That was in the late sixties. In most circles, the "career woman" was no longer viewed as "masculine" or "deviant," but ambitious women were still suspect if their behavior threatened men or made them feel uncomfortable. Mothers of young children were hardest hit, bombarded with "Mother stay home!" messages well into the next decade.

Today, there is widespread recognition that work outside the home is both a personal and an economic necessity for most women. Certainly no self-respecting guy anywhere will stand up and say he's for sex discrimination, or against equal pay for equal work. And while economic discrimination and prejudicial attitudes are still with us, the rigid distinction between "his job" and "her job" has loosened up, for sure.

It's still women, however, who are expected to sacrifice their ambitions and earning power when they conflict with family expectations and pressures. Even today, many women with young children don't feel entitled to pursue career goals, or even to formulate them. Women still tell me about the stress of juggling or balancing work and home, as if this is a personal problem that each woman must solve for herself with the acquisition of new organizational skills and a brighter attitude.

Of course, the problem is real enough, but it's not just a women's issue. Men also need to make sacrifices and trade-offs in their careers to be home more for their families. And the solution can't be achieved through individual effort alone. The structure and policy of organizations

must shift to reflect the most basic of human realities—
that parents need time for their jobs, time for their children, and time for themselves and each other.

Many women tell me that their work is the most
empowering and growth-producing force in their lives. But
work doesn't always go well, and wouldn't even in a world
where discrimination and prejudice magically didn't exist.
Organizations live and die just as families do, and they run
the gamut from the healthy to the dysfunctional.
Furthermore, even the most fair-minded work setting will
begin to act like a crazy family when anxiety is high and
the survival of the institution is at stake.

We, too, may unwittingly make things harder for ourselves. In the early stages of my career, I spoke out without
considering matters of timing and tact, and my attempts to
protest unfairness or to assert my point of view only
elicited criticism or disapproval rather than understanding. Work has always comprised a large percentage of my
waking life, so when it hasn't gone well, neither has my
life. Over the years I learned through experience (the
name we give to our mistakes) to act wisely on my own
behalf.

In the workplace it's more important to be respected
than to be loved. And it's more important to be clear,
direct, and principled than to have a nice day. It doesn't
help to be conflict-avoidant, on the one hand, or too emotional, on the other. The challenge is to communicate
clearly about problems and expectations, to put things in
writing and memos, calmly take a position on issues that
matter, and let the rest go.

Most important, we need to know that we can survive
without a particular job, if need be. This isn't always possible, but we can be as creative as possible in generating new
options. If we're convinced we can't live without our job,
we can't really act on our principles or have a clear bottom
line. Or a very nice day, for that matter.

How Much Do You Make?

Dear Harriet:

What do you think about women telling one another how much money they make? I teach at a local college, and a colleague of mine refused to tell me her salary, even though the information would have helped me to negotiate a pay raise. I thought women were supposed to do things to empower one another! Do you tell other women what you make? Whatever happened to sisterhood?

Dear Reader:

Yes, if we all shared our salaries (men, too), the information would empower us personally, and it would ultimately lead to a fairer world. Women could negotiate pay raises from a position of knowing the facts. We could spot unfairness and discrimination. Bosses would be called on to define clear and objective criteria for who gets paid what. We might even succeed in putting an end to the wage gap between men and women. And we might all have very interesting conversations about how we feel about making "too much" or "too little."

Salaries are part of the public record in government institutions, so if you're working for a city or state college, the information you seek can't be withheld from you. But most people consider their paychecks to be nobody's business but their own. Money is a highly private matter in our culture—a "high twitch" subject, typically discussed even less candidly than sex. If your colleague doesn't have a close relationship with you (and even if she does), she might well have experienced your question as an invasion of her privacy.

Of course, some traditions about what's private deserve to be challenged. The women's liberation move-

> It's naive to think that other women are there to empower you before you have earned their regard and trust.

ment would not have occurred had we not made the private public—and come forth with the most personal accounts of our lives. But an individual woman is unlikely to share sensitive information if she doesn't feel safe doing so. To refuse to reveal one's salary is simply to do what society teaches and, in many cases, what the boss expects, or even requires. And some women are just plain embarrassed by how much or little they make and worry (sometimes realistically) about how others will respond to the facts.

A woman might also fear that revealing her salary would ultimately be used against her. The other person might not use the information discreetly ("I'm furious! Susan just told me that she's making several thousand dollars more than you're paying me"). In some work settings, a woman who tells her salary risks being labeled a troublemaker or otherwise incurring her boss's anger and disapproval.

Some women are financially and emotionally secure enough to take such a risk. Others are not. Job insecurity—and the numerical scarcity of women in high positions—lead to pressures to conform, to fit in, not to rock the boat, and to avoid forming coalitions with other women. Of course, if we eventually want to achieve parity, we should not knuckle under to such pressures. But it's naive to think that other women are there to empower you before you have earned their regard and trust. And the fact is, survival does tend to be a more compelling motivation than sisterhood.

Do I let other women know what I make? Yes, if I have a relationship with the person asking and if I know she won't use the information at my expense. In other cases, even if I don't want to reveal the specific details of my paycheck, I can still provide helpful information and encourage the woman to command a higher salary or fee for the work she does.

My own hope is that we all move toward greater openness when it comes to sharing information about what we make, and that we proceed with maturity and good judgment when we are entrusted with the information others reveal to us. We also need to examine our deepest anxieties about making money. Unlike men, women tend to price ourselves too low, feel grateful for too little, and not ask for more, even when it's there for the asking. We may even feel that trying to make a lot of money is a bad thing.

In any case, you won't enhance the cause of sisterhood by failing to respect your colleague's right to make her own personal decisions about what she will or will not reveal. Sisterhood does not require us to "tell all" but rather to respect our differences. If you can restore the comfort level between you, you'll have other opportunities to support and empower each other, even if her paycheck always remains nobody's business but her own.

I Can't Believe I Was Fired

Dear Harriet:

I worked for fifteen years for a small business that claimed to be like family. But when a financial crisis hit, they not only fired me but were so insensitive and uncaring it took my breath away. Is this how a "family" treats its members? I'm in a state of total shock that my organization didn't find a way to keep me when I've been so loyal.

Dear Reader:

Here's what one of my mentors, family therapist Katherine Kent, taught me some years back: Work is work. Family is family. We should never confuse them, even if our organization does.

It's a terrible shock to be terminated from a job, especially when we don't see it coming. But businesses do not exist to love and care for us. The primary goal of a work organization is to ensure its own economic viability, not to make its employees happy. When an organization is thriving economically, it can sometimes afford the luxury of paying more attention to employee morale and satisfaction. However, organizations live and die just as people do, and when survival anxiety is high, we may discover just how expendable we are.

Of course you deserved to be treated with compassion and caring at the time of your termination. But the moral of the story is this: When a work system makes like it's family, don't believe it.

When the Lady Is Boss

Dear Harriet:

I recently assumed the position of executive director in an almost exclusively male organization. I am feeling under enormous stress, which I attribute to being a woman in a position of authority over men. Could you shed light on some of the particular problems associated with being female and being a boss? How can I combat the sexist attitudes I encounter?

Dear Reader:

Being a boss, irrespective of gender, is a difficult challenge. Being a female boss is more difficult still. Intellectually people may recognize that leadership is a matter of competence and skill, rather than gender. But at the gut level, resistance to female authority runs deep.

The irrational reactions to a woman in power have been summed up as follows: If she is the nurturing sort, she may be called smothering. If she is not so giving, she may be viewed as cold. If she is firm and decisive, she may be seen as masculine and aggressive. If she does not express so-called masculine qualities, she may be thought weak and ineffectual. And if the mixed messages cause her to give up, her failure will be considered proof that a woman can't do the job.

As a woman in a predominantly male work culture, you are a numerically scarce commodity. And research backs up what you yourself are experiencing—that high stress levels go hand in hand with being the minority at work. Numerically scarce individuals of any type are called tokens and face a very distinct set of problems.

What are some of them? Rosabeth Moss Kanter's pioneering research on tokenism points out that tokens are not perceived as individuals but rather as representatives of their kind ("Let's see how a woman handles this position"). As a result, tokens typically end up either conforming to the stereotypes of their group or bending over backward to fight them. In either case it is difficult to relax and behave naturally. Tokens may derive satisfaction from being viewed as special and from occupying a position previously denied to members of their own group. But too often the stresses on tokens far outweigh the gratifications.

As a solo woman, you are in no position to combat sexism or to significantly influence the male culture of your workplace. So don't set yourself up for the impossible by trying to raise the consciousness of your workplace all by yourself. But as executive director of your organization, you can do all you can to hire and promote women. Number balancing does more than any other strategy to combat sexism in group life. In the meantime, connect with other professional women in your community who can offer you company, wisdom, and support.

> At the gut level, resistance to female authority runs deep.

My Boss Is Too Critical

Dear Harriet:

I work in a clothing store. Last week my boss called me into her office and criticized me unfairly, saying that two customers had complained about me. When I tried to tell my side of the story, she accused me of being difficult. I became enraged and pointed out some of her problems in dealing with people. I know I'm right, and I won't play games. But now things are so tense between us that I dread going to work.

Dear Reader:

When it comes to criticism, it is surely more blessed to give than to receive. No one enjoys being on the receiving end of criticism, and it's certainly hardest to handle when we don't agree with it. But criticism, like life itself, is not always fair.

Fair or not, though, the only thing we can control and change is our own behavior. We cannot *not* respond to criticism. Whatever we say—or do not say—will affect what happens next.

Truth may be on your side, but clearly the interaction with your boss moved from bad to worse, so truth isn't really the issue here. What went wrong in the encounter? Since you can't change your boss, concentrate on your part in the downward spiraling sequence. The following "don'ts" might help you to get through more smoothly the next time around:

Don't defend yourself when you're being criticized. Instead, listen respectfully and ask questions. Give yourself time to consider the feedback before telling your side.

Don't criticize a person who is trying to criticize you. Choose another time to voice your grievances and complaints.

Don't state your own position until you can do so calmly, without blaming or putting down the criticizer. When you're feeling intense, remember that old maxim in reverse: "Don't just do something, stand there!" If your fires are rising, you can always say, "I need a little time to think about what you're saying. Could we please set up another time to discuss it further."

Don't bring up everything. Take a clear stand on important issues, and let the rest go.

I respect your wish not to "play games" by seeming to accept your boss's criticism. But a work relationship is *not* an intimate relationship, which does require the spontaneous sharing of real feelings on an equal footing. At work, your boss has the power, and behaving strategically rather than spontaneously isn't dishonest—it's realistic. By choosing your battles and considering matters of timing and tact, you maximize the chances that your boss will consider your point of view.

The more you can put aside your emotional response and focus on the facts, the more likely it is that your boss will do the same. And it's not an insult to your dignity to say, "I'm sorry that something went wrong with those customers. I'll think about how I might handle things differently the next time around." An apology need not be an admission of complete blame but rather a recognition that you might have unwittingly played some part, no matter how small, in a negative interaction.

> At work, behaving strategically rather than spontaneously isn't dishonest—it's realistic.

I'm So Humiliated

Dear Harriet:

I wrote a play that ran for four evenings in Minneapolis, where I live. I know that the audience enjoyed the performance and I got great feedback. But the local newspaper gave it a hateful, humiliating review that devastated me. I feel I'll never write again. How does someone maintain self-esteem when their work is slashed in their own hometown? Each time I read the review I feel angrier and more depressed.

Dear Reader:

Stop rereading that review! File it or trash it, but don't dignify it with another reading.

Almost every writer I know, myself included, has been on the receiving end of a hack-and-slash review. The renowned novelist Margaret Atwood once told an audience of book reviewers, "My work has been written about excellently, disastrously, fairly and intelligently, unfairly and intelligently, well but stupidly, and with an excess of bile, envy, bias, malice and personal hatred that would make you wonder whether perhaps you're a multiple personality and some of the others have been running around torturing small animals and eating babies without your being aware of it."

The only way we can totally protect ourselves from humiliation is by not trying to do anything challenging. But if we want to try to succeed on a grand scale, we take the risk of criticism on a grand scale. Many of us obsess over the unfairness of criticism, when the truth is we remember the criticism long after others have forgotten it—if they even took note of it in the first place. And critics who are nasty enough drown in their own poison.

We might all wish to put on armor (or at least a wet suit) to shore ourselves up against public humiliation. It's understandable that you feel devastated. What has happened to you is no less terrible because it happens frequently. Know that you're in good company and that you *will* write again.

> We might all wish to put on armor
> (or at least a wet suit) to shore ourselves
> up against public humiliation.

Is Volunteer Work a Good Thing?

Dear Harriet:

At a party last week, I was talking about doing volunteer work in a local hospital and at an elementary school. A good friend really put me down, saying that women should be paid for their work and that I was allowing myself to be exploited. The fact is, my husband takes good care of me, and I have no need or desire for paid employment. Was my friend right, or was I justified in being angry?

Dear Reader:

Of course, your friend has a right to her opinions on volunteer work, and you have a right to your anger. But your friend doesn't have the answers to how you should live your life or spend your time. We'd all do well to keep in mind that we can't really know with certainty what is right or best for another person. It is difficult enough to sort these things out for ourselves.

Since this woman is a close friend, let her know that you felt put down by what she said. Close friendships can thrive only when there is room for difference and disagreement; simply let your friend know your position without criticizing or blaming her.

So what about volunteerism instead of paid employment? On the up side, caring, doing for others, and giving freely reflect the best of our female heritage. We may fail to pay due respect to volunteerism because we have learned to undervalue what seems to come naturally to us and to overvalue the competitive, hierarchical, profit-oriented values of the dominant culture.

On the down side, our nation has been built on the unpaid and underpaid work of women, and women have suffered greatly as a consequence. It is also true that power is not equally distributed in traditional marital arrangements, which too often follow the golden rule (he who has the gold makes the rules). Economic disparity in marriage can influence each person's sense of entitlement in decision making, even when we're not aware of it.

> While your husband takes good care of you now, do you have a way to earn a living if that changes?

The reality is that women who are economically dependent on their husbands often become poor after being widowed or divorced. Rather than thinking, *This could never happen to me*, it is wise to have a life plan that considers the hard facts regarding the current divorce rate, the lack of high-level training and reentry programs for displaced homemakers, the low or uncollectible child-care payments, and negligible alimony. Does volunteer work defer or prevent you from considering these facts? While your husband takes good care of you now, it's important for you to consider whether you have a way to earn a living if that changes.

Obviously, no other person can decide how you should invest your energy and time. If you are one husband away from a welfare check, volunteerism may put you in a vulnerable position. If, on the other hand, volunteerism fits into a carefully thought-through plan and is congruent with your own values, priorities, and beliefs, then it obviously has a place in your life. Nor does it need to preclude part-time paid work.

Minding Our Business

Dear Harriet:

Last year I started cleaning house every Wednesday for my next-door-neighbor Bev. Then she started canceling for one reason or another. I always put this day aside, and when she cancels even once a month, I can't make ends meet. I finally got up the courage to insist that she pay me something when she cancels, even if it's just a token. Bev says no,—she won't pay when I don't work. Now we're both angry. Who is wrong here? How can I fix the situation?

Dear Reader:

Your experience is an important reminder to all of us: Whether we are dentists, decorators, or housecleaners, we should establish clear policies *up front* that we and our clients can accept and live with. If we want to renegotiate the service contract or reestablish guidelines, then we need to discuss the options with our clients.

Try to calm down the situation with Bev, especially since you live next door to each other. If you're feeling too angry to talk calmly to her, send her a card to acknowledge your contribution to the tension between the two of you. Then approach Bev respectfully, without criticism or blame. You might say, for example, that you're sorry you didn't think to establish a cancellation policy right from the start but that it's necessary to do so now if you're to continue housecleaning for her. Ask Bev if she's willing to sit down again and talk to you about it.

Take whatever time you need to identify what you are

comfortable with *before* you meet with her. Is it OK with you if Bev cancels without penalty at least 48 hours or 72 hours in advance? Are you willing to compromise if 72 hours is too much for her but 48 hours is not enough for you? Do you want to be paid in full if Bev doesn't cancel within the agreed-upon time? Or would you settle for a flat cancellation fee, say half

> Whatever your line of work, establish clear policies *up front* that you and your clients can accept.

of what she would ordinarily pay you? If Bev insists on her right to cancel at any time without compensating you, do you want to discontinue working for her?

If you're uncertain about where you stand on any detail, talk to other women who clean houses and learn how they handle cancellations. It's fine to be flexible with Bev, but don't make vague requests (like asking for "just a token" payment), and don't agree to anything that will leave you feeling bitter or resentful. If you and Bev are able to reach a new agreement, put the details on paper, and give Bev a copy to prevent any future misunderstanding.

Don't assume that either you or Bev is wrong if you fail to reach a mutually agreeable contract. You have the right to decide what you think is fair and what employment conditions you can agree to and can live with—but as your employer, so does Bev.

I Can't Stand My Supervisor

Dear Harriet:

Six months ago, I began working at a travel agency. I do a good job, but I hate my supervisor. He is a picky control freak who criticizes me for stupid details, like the fact that I return ten minutes late from lunch or that my paperwork is late. Other employees do the same, but he singles me out. The agency is having money problems, and I really think this guy is scapegoating me. When I point this out, he gets defensive. I've started to dread going to work. How can I make the situation better?

Dear Reader:

When an organization is under stress, any one individual can easily become a candidate for an intensely negative focus. So don't raise your hand and volunteer for the job. Here are three suggestions to deintensify your current painful situation.

First, return from lunch on time and meet all your paperwork deadlines. Although these details may seem trivial to you, they're important to your supervisor, who is, after all, higher up in the hierarchy. Until your relationship with him improves, it's in your best interest to follow all the rules and not give your boss any opportunities for criticism.

> Don't tell your supervisor that he's failing to appreciate you. You'll be seen as a complainer.

Second, don't tell your supervisor that he's picking on you, scapegoating you, or failing to appreciate you. You may be entirely correct, but such statements rarely elicit the desired result. Instead, you'll be seen as a complainer.

Third, move toward your supervisor rather than away from him. Ask him questions that allow him to be helpful.

If you abide by the rules and appeal to your supervisor's competence (no one is all bad), he may lighten up over time and begin to appreciate the good quality of your work. Even if you don't stay in the job in the long run, you will have improved the work atmosphere until you do decide to make a change.

I'm Attracted to a Colleague

Dear Harriet:

At work I sense an increasing level of sexual energy between a male colleague and me. We're both married, and I don't believe in having affairs, but he's getting under my skin and I'm worried about becoming obsessed. Will it help to ask him whether he feels it too? Would that help?

Dear Reader:

Help with what? Clarify for yourself what you actually want to accomplish. Be honest. Does part of you want to keep the sexual energy between the two of you alive? You'll probably accomplish this by asking your colleague whether he shares your feelings. But if you truly want to lower the tension, then it may be wiser to talk with your *husband*— not your colleague—about this attraction.

You can shift the situation with your colleague by being a bit more emotionally distant from him and by casually mentioning your husband in conversation as a reminder (to both of you) that you're married. You may not know what his feelings are, or his expectations, but you can control your own complicity in the flirtation.

Sexual attractions outside of marriage are a normal part of everyday life, especially in the workplace. Some folks are able to take attractions lightly and enjoy them without a problem. For others, like yourself, an attraction can become a big deal, and it's good you're aware of that. Rest assured, the situation is unlikely to stay steamy if you decide to cool it down.

Are Women Just a Bunch of Whiners?

Dear Harriet:

My sister says most women are quite well off economically and that we've become a bunch of whiners, especially about money. What do you think?

Dear Reader:

According to the U.S. Bureau of the Census, American women represent two-thirds of all poor adults and face the worst gender-based pay gap in the developed world. More than 80 percent of full-time working women make less than $20,000 per year. Budget cuts during President Reagan's first term pushed nearly 2 million families in which women were head of the household below the poverty line.

Globally, women do 65 to 75 percent of the world's work and produce 45 percent of the world's food. Yet we receive only 10 percent of the world's income and own 1 percent of the world's property. Personally, I think this is worth whining about.

> More than 80 percent of full-time working women make less than $20,000 per year.

My Employee Has a Bad Attitude

Dear Harriet:

I supervise a bright, talented man named Kevin in a county hospital. He has a big ego and doesn't follow rules. He comes to work late and leaves early, a reflection of his feeling that he's "above" our employment regulations. I've talked to him so often about his bad attitude that I feel like his therapist. How can I figure Kevin out and get through to him?

Dear Reader:

If you're feeling like Kevin's therapist, you're way off track. When you supervise or evaluate employees or staff, stick with issues of *policy* and *procedure*. It's not helpful to analyze or diagnose people—unless they're paying you to do so.

Avoid comments like "You seem to think you're above the rules here." Instead try, "It's company policy that employees arrive at 8:30 and leave at 5:00.

> Don't analyze or diagnose your employees. Instead, clarify the rules and consequences.

Last month there were twelve days that you came late or left early. You're bright and talented and we value your work very highly. We don't want to lose you. But you need to decide whether this job is important enough to you that you can arrive and leave on time."

Forget about figuring Kevin out. Instead, formulate a clear plan of action. Do you want to put Kevin on probation? If so, for how long? What are the terms? Communicate the policy to Kevin in a respectful manner that both values his contribution and clarifies the rules and consequences. Many female bosses are sensitive to appearing uncaring, but you're not doing Kevin a favor if you fail to clarify a bottom-line position about what is acceptable and what is not.

I'm Paralyzed by Criticism

Dear Harriet:

I have always wanted to be a writer and each day I put time aside to write poetry or try my hand at a short story. Now, friends are asking to see my work, but I'm afraid to show it to them. I know I'll be paralyzed if they respond negatively to my attempts to express myself. The problem is, I want to get published, but I hate rejection. Would you share your experience with writing? Can anyone learn to write? How can I overcome my fear?

Dear Reader:

If you are feeling too vulnerable to show your work to anyone right now, then don't. Down the road a bit—whether next month or next year—you may feel more prepared to hear others' reactions. At certain points in the creative process we may need to keep our work private because a negative response from others could discourage us, or shut us down altogether. Trust your intuition about when and to whom to show your work.

When you are ready to share your writing, choose your critics with care and make sure they know something about writing. If you feel especially vulnerable, let your readers know that and tell them what would be most helpful. Be clear about your needs. I will sometimes say to a friend, "I'm feeling very shaky about this piece. I want only your most tactful, generous, and supportive response." At another time I may invite a friend to be as critical and blunt as possible.

No one enjoys rejection. The challenge is not to let it stop you. My first book, *The Dance of Anger*, was turned down by countless publishers over a period of several years. I was devastated by the number of rejections I received—enough to wallpaper the largest room in my home. Although I didn't toughen up emotionally, I did keep going. I incorporated the criticisms that made sense to me and listened when more than two readers had a similar reaction. I let the rest of the comments go.

Can anyone write? Writing is an act of self-expression and self-discovery. Like conversation, it is a basic form of human communication rather than the property of a gifted few. As far as I know, there is no writing gene or publishing gene, although—as in all things—some people have a larger share of natural talent and luck than others. People who publish don't have fairy dust sprinkled over them; they are just regular folks.

To be published, however, is only one of many reasons to write. In our product-oriented society, we may forget that the *process* of writing is its own reward, particularly if this is your passion. Also, publication is not an objective measure of worth. As in the rest of life, there is not always justice in the publishing world.

> No one enjoys rejection.
> The challenge is not to let it stop you.

I hope that you *do* share your work when you are ready, because taking criticism is how we learn. Have you considered joining or starting a writer's group? Many women and men out there write and would value the opportunity to share their hopes, fears, desires, ambitions, experience, and, yes, their work.

I'm a Homemaker and Proud of It

Dear Harriet:

I am a full-time homemaker and I hope that my three daughters will follow in my footsteps. I have to say that I'm angry at the women's movement for putting down this important role. What are your thoughts, as a feminist, about the role of the full-time homemaker?

Dear Reader:

Almost all fields of work that are predominantly female are underpaid and undervalued. Homemakers are no exception, and comprise the largest group of unappreciated and economically unprotected working women.

Globally speaking, the unpaid labor of women in the household, if given economic value, would add an estimated one-third or $4 trillion to the world's annual economic output. But homemakers aren't eligible for Social Security, unemployment, or disability benefits. Their work is excluded from the gross national product and isn't considered productive labor. Although homemakers often work long hours, they are said "not to work." But this unfortunate state of affairs reflects patriarchy, not feminism.

> When homemaking is truly valued, men will want to join us in it as equal partners.

It's not feminism, but rather the mainstream media, that has pitted "Moms" and "career women" against each other, deflecting us from working together to ensure the dignity and economic protection of all women. The issue is not, nor has it ever been, whether homemaking is more or less valuable than, say, being an engineer. The real issue is that the role of homemaker places many women in a position of profound economic vulnerability. This vulnerability is fueled by high divorce rates, negligible alimony, low or uncollectible child-support payments, and the lack of high-level training and reentry programs for displaced homemakers.

Motherhood has always been surrounded by an aura of romantic idealization, but mothers aren't truly valued. (As one feminist put it, "A pedestal, like a prison, is a very small space to walk around on.") Being valued is wonderful, and it is essential to our well-being and self-esteem. But being valued is not the same as receiving the symbolic rewards of sentimental and flowery praise. When homemaking is truly valued, mothers and children will be *economically* protected—and men will want to join us in it as equal partners. I, for one, look forward to such a day.

Promotion Anxiety

Dear Harriet:

Six weeks ago, I got a promotion at work with increased responsibility, opportunity, and a big pay raise. Since then I've been feeling on edge and I'm waking up with a lot of anxiety. I've also been fighting almost nonstop with my husband—and my mother, a housewife, too. I really wanted this promotion, and now that I've got it I can't understand why I'm having such a hard time dealing with it.

Dear Reader:

Change is always stressful, even when it's sought after, and women, in particular, have a hard time with success. Unlike men, who learn that "moving up" will enhance their self-esteem and strengthen their relationships, women learn the opposite. Many women unconsciously equate success with the loss of what they currently have and value—loss of approval, loss of attractiveness, even loss of significant relationships.

One young woman I saw in psychotherapy thought she was having a heart attack the afternoon she made a major breakthrough in writing her doctoral dissertation. "Well, that's your punishment for trying to get a Ph.D.," she said to herself. When my own career began to take off, I was convinced that my plane would plummet to the ground in flames every time I left town to give a professional presentation. But I flew anyway, and eventually my fear subsided.

Women receive countless mixed messages about success, from society and the key people in our lives. A husband may genuinely encourage his wife but then react strongly if she starts making more money or garners more status than he does. A mother may say, "Be successful!" but then ignore or undermine her daughter's success, because the mother herself has never been allowed to seek success or even acknowledge the wish for it. Or a father, blocked from recognizing his own ambitions, may be too focused on his daughter's accomplishments, which also makes success emotionally loaded.

> A husband may genuinely encourage
> his wife to succeed but then react strongly
> if she starts making more money than he does.

To understand more about your own mixed response to success, I suggest that you learn more about the legacy of work and achievement in your family. Adult daughters are deeply sensitive to the hardship and unfulfilled longings of the previous generations of women in their families, and embracing privileges and challenges that separate us from the female traditions of the past is never easy or without conflict. In your conversations with your mother and other female relatives, ask questions like: If you had never married and could have started any career early in life, what would you have done? Do you think you would have been successful? What might have stood in your way? Did you (or other family members) have any special talents or ambitions?

If your dad is living, share your dilemma and inquire about his work experience. How has he responded to his promotions (or the lack of them)? How does he view his successes and failures? What messages has he given you over time about achievement and success? What was his work situation when he was the age that you are now?

Talk to your husband as well. Have men in his family married women as professionally successful as yourself? How did such marriages work out? What did he learn about the appropriate roles of men and women from observing his own parents' marriage?

The more family facts you can gather, the more context you will have for understanding your struggle and the less anxious you will feel. And talking openly with others will help you to consider more objectively the pros and cons of your promotion and clarify what truly constitutes success in your own life.

5

≋

No Place
Like Home

Introduction

Before all else, we are daughters or sons. Our relationships with our parents—and with other members of our first family—are the most influential in our lives, and they are never simple. Family connections tend to be intense, even when they appear calm.

Families are not fair, and we don't choose the one we're born or adopted into. Once upon a time, the word *family* evoked an image (however idealized) of a safe haven of nurturance and unconditional love. Today, a family is what many people are "in recovery" from. For some lucky folks, family is the place we can always return to, no matter what, for a sense of comfort, security, and belongingness. For others, the details of family life are wrenching. As Barbara Ehrenreich notes, "Home is all too often where the small and weak fear to lie down and shut their eyes."

Families don't exist in a vacuum. They are embedded in a particular cultural context that affects them in any number of ways. Societal and economic inequalities shape the deepest interior of family life, and painful historical events, like the legacy of slavery, take generations to work through. What's unresolved in one generation will be reenacted in the next, and there is no "ideal" family that can provide the perfect emotional climate for the unfolding our so-called true selves.

As adults, it's up to us to decide how we will conduct ourselves with those difficult folks the universe has dealt us. We can take the hard route and work toward being *who we are* with family members, without trying to change or convince them to see things our way. We can learn to ask clear questions about our family history and take a calm position when differences arise, without getting defensive or attacking. Or, alternatively, we can go the easy route and stay on automatic pilot, yo-yoing back and forth between distance and blame.

When things get intense in family relationships, it typically looks like this: First, we confront family members by telling them what's wrong with them and how they should think, feel, or behave differently. We confuse our anxiety-driven confrontations with some act of higher virtue on our part, and we blame the other party for being defensive and unable to hear us. We then conclude, with God or our therapist on our side, that our mother (or father, or sister, or Uncle Charlie) can't change and it's best to give up on them. Heck, that's a lot easier than figuring out how we might behave differently, or approach a difficult subject with a bit more timing and tact, or see things from a different angle.

Of course, distancing can bring short-term relief by freeing us from the intense feelings that are stirred by closer contact. At particular points in our lives, seeking distance can even be essential and life-preserving. But if our only option is to stay cut off forever, there is a long-term cost. Whatever goes unresolved and unaddressed with our family of origin will go underground and then pop up somewhere else, especially if we start a family of our own.

People, like other growing things, do not hold up well in the long run when severed from their roots.

Working on family relationships is the royal road to change. It's not that we have to *like* all these folks, or to reconnect with any one of them before we are ready. But if we can learn more about who these people are, and the forces that shaped them, we'll begin to navigate family relationships with greater maturity and balance. This puts us on more solid emotional footing for all our relationship ventures, in both love and work. Even if all we can do right now is send a postcard to Mother's great-aunt Sally, or pay a brief visit to one of the "easier" relatives on our family tree, it helps to move in the direction of more family connectedness over time.

In our society much is made about the importance of achieving *independence* from our family of origin. But what does this word mean? It means that we can stay connected to other family members while remaining ourselves. It means that we can take a clear position on emotionally important issues without having to change, convince, or fix others who see things differently. It's the largest of all human challenges—this business of maintaining both the "I" and the "we" without losing either when the going gets rough.

If we can learn to view our parents and siblings a bit more calmly and objectively—and observe our own part in escalating family patterns that keep us stuck—then our other relationships will be a piece of cake.

My Brother's Gay—and I'm Worried

≈≈

Dear Harriet:

My younger brother is gay and in college. I totally accept his sexual orientation, but I can't help feeling sorry for him. First, he will never be given a chance to make a significant contribution to society. Second, I'm terrified he'll get the gay disease, meaning AIDS. Finally, he will face profound discrimination. Given this reality, who would want to be homosexual?

Dear Reader:

The reality you describe may be based more on your feelings than on facts. Why do you assume your brother will not have a chance to make a contribution? From the beginning of recorded time, gay men have achieved extraordinary prominence. A list of prominent gay men would include Socrates, Francis Bacon, Hans Christian Andersen, Walt Whitman, Horatio Alger, Oscar Wilde, Marcel Proust, and Jean Cocteau, to name just a few. The contributions of gay men to history and culture are incalculable. In fact, as a heterosexual woman, you may have a harder time making it into the history books than your brother.

> Don't assume that your gay brother would want to be heterosexual if he had a choice.

As for AIDS, it is a terrifying epidemic, but it is not exclusively a gay disease. Heterosexual transmission is common, and anyone who engages in unsafe sex is vulnerable.

Yes, gays and lesbians do face terrible discrimination. But so do African-Americans and other oppressed groups. African-Americans may feel despairing about racism, but not about their color and cultural heritage. Few African-Americans would choose to become white, despite the enormous privilege that white skin confers. Don't take it as a given that your brother would wish to be heterosexual.

Your feeling sorry for your brother suggests that you may not be as accepting of his sexual orientation as you would like to think, and that's understandable. Total acceptance of homosexuality requires us to unlearn a lifetime of misinformation and cultural indoctrination. Consider learning more about gay culture and at some point working actively for gay and lesbian rights. Your despair may ultimately be replaced by hope and pride.

My Mother Wants to Live with Me

≈≈

Dear Harriet:

My seventy-nine-year-old mother wants to leave her home in South Carolina to come live with me in Maine. Her good friends have all moved away or died, and she feels lonely. But I know she would be miserable in my apartment. She dislikes animals (I have two cats), she dreads the cold, and she hates my music. Unfortunately, though, she denies that she would be bored and lonely living with me. When I was a child, my grandpa moved in with us until his death, and she's convinced that she should do the same with me. How can I make her realize that she will be unhappy if she moves? She's as stubborn as a mule.

Dear Reader:

Don't assume you know what's best for your mother. Perhaps she would happily (or unhappily) endure the cats, the cold, and the music in exchange for the comfort of living with her daughter. Stop trying to convince her to see things your way. It's impossible to change her mind (you've already tried), and you can't know for sure what's best for her.

Instead, examine your own beliefs. What would it be like to have your mother sharing your apartment? If her health declined or her needs increased, what would you be willing to do for her? Have you lived as an adult with your mother for an extended time, and, if so, what was your experience? How much do you want your space?

If you don't want this move to happen, tell your

mother why it won't work for you without disqualifying her perspective. For example:

> Mom, I know that you want to live with me. The problem is that I've grown to love having my own place and, to be honest, it would just be too difficult for me to live with my mother again, even though I love you very much. I'm also worried that if you moved here, I would feel totally responsible for you, even if you asked me not to.

Family members tend to hold very different beliefs about what is selfish and what is a reasonable claim to self-hood. If your mother responds with hurt and upset at your decision, do your best to keep the conversation going.

For example, ask your mother to tell you more about what it was like for her to take care of her dad. What was difficult? What was rewarding? Has she always expected that you would care for her the same way? How disappointed is she that you are not able to do this for her? Don't back off from the real emotional issue between you, which may have to do with the different ways that you and your mother perceive matters of family responsibility.

Our society as a whole has failed to find a caring way to meet the needs of elderly persons. What is unresolved and unattended to at the societal level may surface intensely in the intimate lives of mothers and daughters. It can't be easy for your mother to have suffered so many losses and to face growing older alone.

> Mothers and daughters may have very different opinions about what constitutes family responsibility.

If living with you isn't an option, help your mother to think about other alternatives. Would you consider the possibility of your mother being closer without moving in, say, living in a retirement home in your town? If not, will you help her to explore what resources are available to her in South Carolina? Enlist other family members in the discussion, because as your mother's needs increase, you won't be able to be helpful to her all by yourself.

There is no blueprint to help you sort out your responsibility for yourself and your responsibility to your mother. Over time, let your mother know what you can and can't do for her; and in return respect her competence, her stubbornness, and her right to see things differently.

My Sister Won't Quit Smoking

Dear Harriet:

My diabetic sister, Joanne, has gone back to heavy smoking after having quit three years ago. She is doing this against medical advice and at great risk to her health. I have tried everything to get her to stop. Last month I told her that I will not visit her or bring my children to her house if she doesn't quit. As things now stand we are both angry at each other and she says I'm not welcome in her home. My friends are telling me to forget it and leave her alone, but I feel like she's killing herself. Am I wrong?

Dear Reader:

It's understandably painful to watch your sister jeopardizing her health. But Joanne undoubtedly knows about the hazards of smoking, and as an adult she needs to clarify her own priorities, make her own choices, and take her own chances. While you might wish her to choose otherwise, she is in charge of her body and her life.

> Rest assured that the more you try to fix her, the more likely she is to dig in her heels.

Your feelings of concern are not "wrong"—we all have a right to what we think and feel. But it's not your job to get your sister to shape up or to convince her to see things your way. And rest assured that the more you try to change her, the more likely she is to dig in her heels. The way things are going, you may lose your sister emotionally long before you lose her physically. Refusing to visit Joanne is heading toward cutoff—which won't benefit anyone, your children included.

Consider calming things down by apologizing to your sister for your failure to appreciate that this is her life, not yours. And while the reasons for her to quit may seem overwhelmingly obvious to you, there's no way for you to appreciate fully the purposes that smoking serves for Joanne and the forces that prevent her from stopping at this time.

This is not to say that you should forget it and say nothing. You can share your thoughts and feelings with your sister without returning to your earlier I-know-what's-best position. For example:

> Joanne, I've been feeling terrible about the tension between us and I want to apologize for my part in it. It's incredibly painful for me to think that my children and I may never be welcome in your home and that I have brought this on with my own behavior. I hope you will forgive me for coming on like a ton of bricks about the smoking. It's just that I'm terribly afraid of losing you. I want you to be around as long as possible, both as a sister for me and as an aunt to my kids. I think that's why I've been so intense. Although my fear stays with me, I recognize that it's not my job to tell you what to do.

If the two of you are hardly on speaking terms, it may be best to drop Joanne a note, which you can later follow up with a call. Remember, the challenge is not in prolonging your sister's life (which you cannot control anyway) but in working on having a good relationship with her while you are both around.

Coping with a Suicide in the Family

Dear Harriet:

Two years ago my younger brother David killed himself on his twenty-second birthday. My mother is still overcome with guilt and remorse. To be honest, she has good reason to feel responsible for David's death, because she always criticized him and then cut him off entirely for several years. Could she have caused his suicide?

Dear Reader:

A suicide is a profoundly devastating event that sends emotional shock waves through a family for years, decades, and even generations to come. Every family member needs help dealing with this traumatic loss—not just your mother.

Mothers are often the hardest hit by the death of a child, and your family may be no exception. Your mother—like all parents—might have made mistakes in parenting for which she rightfully feels guilty. But she is not responsible for your brother's death. If anyone bears the ultimate responsibility for David's suicide, that person is David.

Countless children grow up in families where they are subjected to unspeakable violence and rejection, and the majority of these children do not respond by killing themselves. Furthermore, suicide—like any dysfunctional or desperate behavior—also occurs in the most loving families.

Although numerous theories are put forth on the cause of suicide, we know relatively little about the complex, multiple factors that predispose a particular individual to suicidal behavior. We do know that suicide is not "caused" by one family member, nor can it be understood by focusing narrowly on a particular family relationship. Similarly, a family member cannot keep alive someone who is determined to die.

In the aftermath of suicide, or any other tragedy or untimely loss, it is normal for family members to ask who's to blame. Blaming can be overt or it can be subtle and indirect. Because those left to deal with a loved one's suicide can never obtain all the facts or reconstruct the complete picture, fantasies about its cause will flourish wildly. You might benefit from consulting a family systems therapist. This process can help you move away from distancing and blaming so that you gain a more objective perspective on David's suicide and support one another at this difficult time.

> If anyone is responsible for your brother's suicide, that person is your brother.

Your local mental health association can also put you in touch with groups like Compassionate Friends and the American Association of Suicidology, which offer valuable information and support. Compassionate Friends, an organization founded for bereaved parents, has expanded to include siblings and other family members. Your mother might also seek help for herself. Approximately 50,000 people a year commit suicide in the United States; your mother isn't alone in her feelings of profound guilt and grief.

Should I Cross Dad Off My Wedding List?

Dear Harriet:

As I plan my wedding, I'm faced with having to choose which of my parents to include. Even though they have been divorced for seven years, my mom still refuses to be in the same room with my dad, and says that if I invite him, she won't come. Both of my parents are important to me, but I've always felt closer to my mother and I'd be devastated if she didn't come. What should I do?

Dear Reader:

Your mother and father are legally but not emotionally divorced, which is *their* problem, not yours. Neither you—nor your parents—will benefit if you side with one at the expense of the other. We all need to work on having a relationship with each parent that is separate from the conflicts between the two parents.

Consider inviting both your parents to your wedding. Let each of them know that their presence is important to you. Tell your mother how very much you want her there and how incredibly important she is to you, but don't tell her what to do. If she blames you for inviting your father,

> Weddings are predictably anxious times in families and often cause existing conflicts to intensify or even explode.

then restate your position as often as necessary but without becoming critical or defensive.

You might say, for example, "Mom, the older I get, the more I realize how much my family means to me. I know that many painful things have happened between you and Dad, but it's just too difficult for me to pretend that I don't have a father. I love you both, and I couldn't leave one of you off my invitation list for the most important celebration of my life."

Weddings are predictably anxious times in families and often cause existing conflicts to intensify or even explode. Your mother may indeed choose to avoid your wedding—or she may turn her anger against you. Try to see your mother's reaction as nothing more than her way of managing anxiety and let her know that you understand how hard your decision is for her. The challenge for you is to avoid managing your own anxiety by attacking back—or by excluding any significant family member from your wedding.

A Helping Hand

Dear Harriet:

My older sister, Cara, just called me and said that she was depressed about not having a clear direction in her life. She has never shared a serious problem with me before, and I found myself not knowing how to respond to her obvious distress. What can I do?

Dear Reader:

What is your intuitive sense about how to help Cara? Does she simply want you to listen, nod supportively, and ask questions about her problem? Would she like to hear how you have struggled with similar issues in your own life? Would she like advice? Would she feel reassured if you expressed

> If you want to know how to be most helpful to your sister—ask her.

confidence in her ability to solve the problem over time—or would she feel you were offering false reassurance and minimizing her struggle? Would she like you to distract her when she's feeling down?

The only way to be certain about what Cara will find supportive is to ask her. Usually, the most helpful thing we can do for distressed family members is to care about them—to be emotionally present without pulling back from their pain and without trying to fix it.

I Miss My Mother

Dear Harriet:

I'm a college student. My mom died in a car accident three years ago at the age of forty-six. I'm getting on with my life OK, but I still think about her. I burst into tears when something reminds me of her and I feel terrible that I didn't ask her so many questions. I read that it takes two years to get over a loss, so why hasn't the pain gone away?

Dear Reader:

Time will dull the edge of grief, but the loss of a mother is an emotional event of such proportions that we don't just "get over it" after a prescribed period of time. When a mother dies prematurely and unexpectedly, as yours did, her death is more painful yet.

The writer Anna Quindlen writes about the loss of her own mother:

> My mother died when I was 19. For a long time, it was all you needed to know about me, a kind of vest-pocket description of my emotional complexion. "Meet you in the lobby in 10 minutes—I have long brown hair, am on the short side, have on a red coat, and my mother died when I was 19. . . ." Sometimes I feel like one of those people searching for the mother who gave them up for adoption. I have some small questions for her, and I want the answers. How did she get her children to sleep through the night? Was there olive

oil in her tomato sauce? Was she happy? If she had it to do over again, would she?

Give yourself permission to mourn your mother without impatience or self-criticism, and expect emotional ripples or even tidal waves to hit you years down the road. You may miss your mom acutely at your college graduation, your wedding, the birth of your first child, when you reach the age your mother was when she died, and when your daughter reaches the age you were when you lost your mom. You may miss her on her birthday, her death day, and Mother's Day. You may miss her, as Quindlen says, when you stand in your kitchen when you are in your forties and wonder how she made her spaghetti sauce.

> The loss of a mother is an emotional event of such proportions that we don't just "get over it."

Expect emotional upheaval as well as shifts in all your family relationships. Try to stay connected to surviving family members who can support you in your grief and also to members of your mom's family who can provide you with stories and facts about her over time.

It's especially helpful to talk to other women who have lost their mothers to learn how they experienced their mother's death and coped with their loss over time. Such conversations and connections will offer you comfort, insight, wisdom, and the understanding that you're not alone.

My Brother-in-Law
Made a Pass at Me

Dear Harriet:

My sister, Lila, has been married to Reuben for ten years. Reuben and I had a good relationship until he made a pass at me a while ago. I got furious at him and thought that would be the end of it. However, the last time I visited them, he put his arm around me and tried to kiss me. I feel I have to tell my sister, but I'll feel guilty if my telling her wrecks their marriage.

Dear Reader:

Since you have a relationship with your brother-in-law, I suggest that you talk to him first and ask him what he thinks is going on. Let him know that you can't keep such a big secret from your sister, because it creates too much distance between the two of you. He may want to tell Lila before you do.

If you end up talking to your sister, give her the facts and express your concern that the news will wreck her marriage. Let her know that you hope she

> Silence can pose a greater threat than the difficult truth.

and Reuben can struggle through this together and make sense of it. Share this information without interpreting, condemning, or telling Lila what to do.

Reuben's inappropriate behavior sounds like it may have little to do with you personally or even with sexual attraction itself. Rather, he may be creating a crisis that will force him to examine the real sources of stress in his life that are contributing to his sabotaging his marriage. Although he may become angry with you for bringing his behavior out into the open, don't distance yourself from either Lila or Reuben as they struggle to work on their relationship with each other and with you.

Your decision to spill the beans is a responsible one. Silence can pose a greater threat than the difficult truth. Family relationships are most at risk when we "protect" others from important facts that affect them, and when difficult emotional issues stay beneath the surface and can't be talked about.

My Distant Dad

Dear Harriet:

My workaholic father and I never had much of a relationship when I was growing up. After my mother died and he retired, our relationship became even more distant. Last week, my husband and I drove 500 miles to visit him with our new baby (our first!), and I confronted my dad about the fact that we never talk about anything important. I told him that I really want to feel close to him but that his silence is uncaring. He got defensive, I got angry, and the visit ended on a sour note. I feel totally frustrated. Please help.

Dear Reader:

You're not alone in your feelings. It is often difficult for daughters to feel close to their fathers. In many families, Dad is in the distant, odd-man-out position. Fathers sometimes don't know how to be close, particularly if they were raised in families where their own dads were absent or emotionally unavailable.

The problem you describe doesn't indicate a lack of love or caring on your dad's part. It's just a common family pattern that is deeply rooted in the roles and rules of our culture. Such patterns change only slowly, over time. Trying to do too much too fast often gives us a great excuse to give up and do nothing at all ("You see, he's impossible!"). And pursuing intimacy, like commanding someone to be spontaneous, has a paradoxical effect, because the other party, feeling anxious and at a loss, may withdraw even more.

Keep in mind that the visit with your dad occurred at an emotionally intense time for both of you because it followed on the heels of an important life-cycle event—the birth of your first child. At such emotionally loaded times, we tend to revert even further into reflexive patterns that block the possibility of intimacy. For example, you pursue your dad for closeness, he distances; you blame, he distances more, and so it goes. Pursuing, distancing, and blaming are normal ways of navigating relationships under stress, but they also keep us stuck.

> Try as we may, we can't orphan ourselves. The intensity we avoid by cutting off from a parent just pops up somewhere else.

So where to begin? For starters, try to bring the anxiety down a bit, creating a calmer emotional field in which change can happen. You might write your dad a chatty letter with news about the baby, commenting briefly and noncritically on the tension between the two of you: "Dad, I felt some tension between us during our last visit and I want to apologize for my part in it. I think that I felt awkward—although I didn't realize it at the time—because I was missing Mom and wishing she was there to see the baby. In any case, it was good to see you and to have my baby meet his grandfather!" Avoid lengthy, heavy psychologizing.

What next? We move toward genuine closeness when we share more about the self over time. Stay in good contact with your dad, share your own news, and invite him in turn to share his wisdom, experience, and expertise with you. Work on becoming a good questioner. You can begin with neutral subjects: "Dad, we're thinking of taking a trip to Chicago. What should we see while we're there?"

Later, when the comfort level is higher, you can address emotionally important subjects: "Dad, I'm really struggling with the question of going back to work. I've been wondering about how you made the decision to start your own business. I also couldn't remember whether Mother ever struggled with wanting a career or job outside the home while she was raising us kids."

Learning more about your dad's family is also a good way to get to know both him and yourself better. The more you can question him calmly and with genuine respect, the more likely it is that your dad will find the emotional space to respond. But if you comment directly on the distance between you ("Dad, I'm really sad that we're not closer"), then your dad is likely to become more anxious and defensive. Take it slowly. Substantive change in family relationships sometimes requires us to move at glacial speed.

So why bother? Many of us don't. But I encourage you to accept the challenge. If you work on becoming more connected to your dad, then you'll gain a firmer footing in your other intimate relationships. Try as we may, we can't orphan ourselves. The intensity we avoid by cutting off from a parent just pops up somewhere else. Successfully navigating relationships within our own family of origin is the most valuable legacy that we leave our children.

Is My Sister a Lesbian?

Dear Harriet:

My younger sister, Amber, who is twenty-six years old, has told us she's a lesbian. She says she is in love with a woman for the first time in her life. Until now, she has dated and slept with only men. I think she's just going through a phase and isn't really homosexual. But when my mother and I both told Amber that we could not refer to her as a lesbian because we don't believe she is one, she became furious. Do you think Amber is a lesbian and that she'll be this way for the rest of her life? What causes homosexuality and what makes a person "gay" or "straight"?

Dear Reader:

We all tend to simplify our world by thinking in terms of dichotomous categories: good and evil, masculine and feminine, yin and yang, heterosexual and homosexual. But people are complex, multifaceted, and changeable. Many individuals do fit neatly into the category of either gay or straight—and stay there for a lifetime. But many do not.

What will Amber's sexual orientation be ten years from now? Without a crystal ball, it is impossible to know for sure. Falling in or out of love with another woman (or just plain experimenting) can happen at any stage of the life cycle. The Kinsey Institute reports that around one-half of college-educated women (and about 20 percent of non-college-educated women) have had at least one same-sex erotic encounter since puberty. Its research has also found that approximately 10 percent of the population has a basic same-sex orientation. Other estimates suggest that

approximately one in every five families has a child who
falls (or will someday fall) into the category of homosexual. Lesbians and gays are everywhere, despite our society's
tendency to deny their right to love openly or even to exist.

We do not know what causes homosexuality any more
than we know what causes heterosexuality, but we do know
that homosexuality is as normal as heterosexuality. To that
end, the American Psychiatric Association struck homosexuality from its manual of psy-
chiatric disorders in 1973.

> Dealing with
> differences is the
> greatest of all human
> challenges.

Is Amber a lesbian? She
loves a woman and she calls
herself a lesbian. Naming
ourselves is an important
empowering process and it's
understandable that she would feel hurt to have you deny
her right to do so. Perhaps you and your mother can learn
to respect Amber's choice of language because it has
meaning for her.

Of course, this isn't to say that your feelings of confusion and concern aren't also understandable. When an
individual announces that she or he is lesbian or gay, the
news inevitably sets off a chain of anxious rumblings in
other family members. The real issue is how relationships
in your family will shift because of this new information
and how openly you can talk about your reactions to
Amber's self-disclosure.

Explore what the word *lesbian* means to your sister,
your mother, and you. Various forces have shaped your
reactions and associations with the word, whose meaning
may have changed over time for some of you. How long,
for example, did it take Amber to acknowledge and accept
her love for another woman? It may help both of you to
have honest, nonaccusatory conversations about your
respective feelings, fears, and beliefs.

Will other family members be able to accept Amber's

relationship? Will any family members now distance themselves from Amber, or perhaps even cut her off? Has any
member of your family—including anyone from past generations—ever been excluded because of his or her difference? How does Amber see the hardships and joys of
being in a lesbian partnership? What will be most difficult
for you about having a gay sister?

Dealing with differences is the greatest of all human
challenges. And since a woman's love for another woman
is a difference that can inspire deep anxiety in some people, family relationships are at risk for anger and estrange-
ment. The challenge for your family is not to let this happen.

My Parents Can't Stand My Boyfriend

≋

Dear Harriet:

I'm twenty-two years old, single, and living rent-free in my parents' terrific basement apartment. Last spring I began to date Ira, a musician my parents can't stand. I've tried to convince them that Ira is wonderful, but now they tell me I'll have to move out if I keep seeing him. We've been fighting nonstop. I think I should have the right to make decisions about my own life. How can I get my parents to treat me like an adult?

Dear Reader:

Of course you have the right to make decisions about your own life. But it's your parents' right to decide what they will tolerate under their own roof and under what conditions they will offer their adult daughter financial support.

You may disagree with their terms, but you can't change or convince your parents. The only person you *can* change is yourself. If you want to live your life as an adult, establish your economic independence from your parents. You're not free to make your own choices if you depend economically on another person and if there is no way to carry on without that financial support.

> Negotiating the balance of separateness
> and togetherness with our first family
> is a lifelong task.

Leaving home may require you to lower your standard of living, but it can also be your ticket to growing up. Perhaps this is the real issue. When a child of any age gets launched, all family members are called upon to redefine their relationships and their sense of self. Fighting with your parents (while you live in their basement) may paradoxically be a way of protecting your folks—and yourself—from the anxiety of change by remaining their little girl.

Don't try to persuade your parents that Ira is a terrific guy. Ira's good and bad points are not the issue. The real issue is how you navigate your separateness and independence from your parents, and how you meet the challenge of staying connected to them while staying yourself. To this end, learn to state your own position without getting critical or defensive. Here's an example: "You know, Mom, every time we talk about Ira, we end up in a fight. It's as if you and Dad can only see the bad in him and I can only see the good. I'm sorry for my contribution to the tension. I think I'm scared that you or Dad will distance yourselves from me or cut me off if I don't agree with you. Of course, I understand that this is your house and you make the rules. But when you say move out or stop seeing Ira, I think you're saying we all have to agree in order to have a relationship. Obviously, we're different people and sometimes we're going to see things differently. I hope we can love and support each other even when we don't agree."

Staying calm, staying connected, and staying true to oneself in the face of differences is perhaps the greatest of all human challenges. Negotiating the balance of separateness and togetherness with our first family is a lifelong task.

Change is never easy, but you're unlikely to move forward if you continue to blame your parents, try to change them, or settle even further into their basement apartment when you don't want to abide by their rules.

A Death in the Family

Dear Harriet:

My father is dying of cancer that is quickly spreading. I want to reach out to my father, but my mom forbids me even to mention the word *cancer* to him. She claims he can't deal with it. I think my mother's silence is destructive, and I wish she would stop playing games. Now we're furious at each other. How can I handle my mom? How do I say good-bye to my dad? Is there a positive way for a family to deal with something as awful as death?

Dear Reader:

Death can overload even the most resilient families. An impending loss stirs up so much anxiety that family members may divide into opposing camps, or become overfocused on what someone else is doing wrong and underfocused on themselves.

Your most important challenge is to respect your mom's different coping style. She will handle the impending loss of her husband in her own way. You need to clarify how *you* want to relate to your dad at this time while respecting the right of other family members to think, feel, and behave in whatever way works for them at this difficult time.

To this end, take the initiative to ease the emotional tensions between you and your mom. Admitting to your part in the problem may help calm things down. You could say, for example, "Mom, I'm sorry that I've contributed to the tension between us. I guess it's easier for me to fight with you than to face losing Dad." You can also apologize for acting as if you have the answers for your mother: "I'm sorry for trying to tell you how to deal with Dad. I'm certainly not the expert, and he's your husband. It's hard enough for me to figure out what I need to do."

At a calm time, you may also want to ask your mother about her reactions to losing her life partner. What changes does she anticipate in her life? What are her biggest fears for the years to come? How does she think her relationships with her siblings, relatives, and friends will change after her husband is gone? Think about how *your* relationship with your mom will shift after your dad's death.

There is no one best way for families to cope with impending death or its aftermath. During a time of imminent loss, the ideal situation would be for family

> Our silence isolates the dying person who knows that people are talking *about* him, not *to* him.

members to have open hearts and open conversations. Everyone would feel free to express a complex range of emotions, including anger, guilt, fear, frustration, helplessness, and sadness. Family members would be able to share their thoughts and feelings without needing others to respond in a particular way.

But more typically, family members, including the dying individual, "protect" one another by concealing painful facts and feelings. Such avoidance makes people comfortable in the short run, but it can ultimately lead to profound emotional isolation, particularly for the dying person who knows people are talking *about* him, not *to* him.

It may help to realize that avoiding the subject of death is usually more for the comfort of the healthy than the dying. People who are dying are usually relieved when others take the initiative to be open and direct. They may appreciate the opportunity to discuss any number of death-related subjects: the music they want at their funeral, their philosophy of death, the meaning and value they attach to their life, and their concerns about the family members they are leaving behind.

If you want to communicate more openly with your dad, stay emotionally connected to him. Spend time alone with him and don't be afraid to talk about the fact that he's dying. You might, for example, ask him direct questions: "Dad, what is the doctor telling you about your prognosis and the course of the cancer?" "Do you agree with the doctors?" You can also ask questions to let him know that you're interested in his thoughts and feelings about his life and his impending death.

If your dad is a private person who doesn't easily share feelings, don't bulldoze him with your own agenda. The challenge is not to pressure him to open up, but rather to be real with him. You don't have to accomplish much in one conversation or cover a large territory in the time you have left. Try to maintain close emotional contact and think about what you most want to share with him.

And if your mom criticizes your behavior, don't strike back. Avoid arguments about who's right or what's true. Stick to nonblaming "I" language: "Mom, I need to say good-bye to Dad in my own way. I'm not saying that my way is right for you or for anyone else. But you and I are two different people. It makes sense that we would handle things differently."

Family relationships may be tense or difficult for a year or two following your dad's death. In the anxious emotional field that surrounds loss, family members frequently swing back and forth between distance and blame. Do the best you can to stay connected with your mom, your extended family, your friends, and whatever community resources are available to you at this difficult time.

My Sister's Husband Is Abusive

Dear Harriet:

My younger sister Ann is married to a man, Joe, who abuses her physically and emotionally. He hasn't hurt her badly yet, but he will. She has left him twice, but each time she's gone back, despite my pleas that she leave him for good. She no longer listens to me, because she says I don't understand her. What can I do to help her get rid of this terrible man? Or should I do what she says and stay away?

Dear Reader:

Sometimes our efforts to fix things for other family members only serve to perpetuate the problem. But this doesn't mean you should stay silent, stay away, or ignore the seriousness of what is happening.

Instead of distancing yourself from Ann, stay in close contact with her and tell her how *you* feel. Speak to your concern about safety while respecting Ann's loyalty to her husband.

You could say, for example, "Ann, when you tell me how intense things get between you and Joe, I feel terrified. It's unbearable to think of you in an unsafe situation, and I'm frightened that one day Joe will really hurt you. I know that this is your life and not mine, but I love you and I worry that you put both yourself and Joe at risk when you don't protect yourself from being hurt and don't insist that Joe get help before you move back in with him."

If your sister is in danger of being harmed, have you let key family members and Ann's closest friends know of this risk to her safety? Even as her sister, you cannot help

Ann all by yourself, and your own level of anxiety will be unbearable if you keep such a secret. Moreover, Ann is most likely to get caught in a downward spiral of abuse if she is cut off from family and friends who do not have the facts. People who love Ann can help her problem-solve without shaming her for staying with someone who gets out of control.

> It may be far more frightening for your sister to leave her husband than to stay with him.

You can stop pleading with Ann yet still communicate your feelings about violence. You might share your belief that there is nothing a woman can do that justifies her being hit and that you don't think anyone should stay in an unsafe situation. At the same time, you can empathize with Ann about how important Joe is to her and her fear of being without him. It may be far more frightening for Ann to leave Joe than to stay with him. Perhaps it will help Ann to know that she has more of a chance of protecting the marriage if she protects herself.

At a calm time, talk with Ann about the options she has when Joe becomes abusive. Does she know in concrete terms what you and others are willing to do to support her? Has she thought about where she would go if she had to get out of the house in the middle of the night? Does she have the telephone number of a battered-women's shelter? Is she aware that she can seek safety in the shelter without filing an official complaint against Joe?

You can also establish a clear position about violence without returning to your earlier I-know-what's-best-for-you stance. For example, if you ever witness violence between Joe and your sister, or if she phones you while it is happening, you can call the police. Explain your decision to Ann: "Ann, you may be right that Joe gets angrier when the police come. But if I did nothing while you were being hurt, I'd feel like I was part of the problem."

When was the last time you shared *your* problems with Ann and asked for *her* reactions? Do you ever call Ann when *you* are having a bad day and need a sisterly shoulder to lean on? Taking such steps may not help Ann leave Joe, but they can help you restore balance in your relationship with her, reminding her that you need her as much as she needs you.

Ultimately, Ann's dilemma reflects something much larger than her private, individual struggle. Violence against women permeates our culture in countless forms. From the dark alley to the Pentagon, we all live in fear of violence. If the entire human family is not working actively toward solutions, we are all part of Ann's problem.

Going Solo

Dear Harriet:

I'm in my late twenties, love my career, and have no wish to marry. My mother says she worries that I will end up old and alone. I personally don't think this is reason enough to look for a husband, but she's constantly on my back. Refusing to talk to her about my single status hasn't made her quit. What do you suggest?

Dear Reader:

We all need to be loved and cared for in our old age, but you're right, that's not a terrific reason to marry. The high divorce rate aside, most married women give far more caretaking than they receive. And even the most nurturing of husbands tend to die first.

From ages sixty-five to seventy-four, roughly half of the entire female population is married. Over age seventy-five, only 24 percent of women still have husbands, although 69 percent of men in this age group have wives. We women need to create a rich network of relationships throughout our lives and not put all our eggs in the basket of marriage. We also need to bring about vast changes in institutional and social policies so that our society becomes truly responsive to the needs of the elderly.

But policy talk aside, if you're really committed to forging a new pattern with your mother, move *toward* the subject of marriage, not away from it. Approach her at a time when you can really listen and ask her to share more about her worst fears about your not marrying. Try to sit in the hot seat and ask lots of questions without defending yourself or taking things personally.

Learn about the single women on your family tree, how they fared, and how other family members felt about them. Ask your mother how she thinks life would have gone for her if she hadn't found a husband. What career would she have chosen if all options had been open to her?

> We women need to create a rich network of relationships throughout our lives. Even the most nurturing of husbands tend to die first.

It might also be revealing for you to discuss with your mother *her* thoughts about growing old. If she is married, how does she perceive her options if *she* becomes widowed and unable to care for herself? Your mother will grow old before you do. Perhaps her real but unspoken worry is who will take care of her in her old age.

False Promises

Dear Harriet:

My mother has had a series of minor strokes and her health continues to worsen. She still lives independently and dreads the idea of a nursing home. She has extracted a promise from my husband and me that this will never happen. In truth, my husband and I could not tolerate her living with us for more than a week and our financial resources are limited. My husband thinks I should be honest with my mother. I think lying will allow her some peace in the present. What do you think?

Dear Reader:

I think that your mother deserves an honest response. She has the right to consider her future based on facts, no matter how difficult. Misinformation or missing information may offer her short-term relief, but lies erode trust and carry a long-term cost. Entering a nursing home—should it come to that—will be all the more devastating if she was promised that she would never have to.

You don't have to hit your mother over the head with dire predictions and worst-case scenarios. You can promise her that you will work with her to explore every alternative to a nursing home, short of moving her in with you. Invite her to think with you about her options, should the time come when she is unable to care for herself.

If you have siblings, engage them in the conversation as well. Involving them directly may lighten your burden and provide your mother with additional perspectives. You can also get in touch with resources in your community that can provide information about in-home care.

Consider all possibilities. But be clear with your mother about what you can and can't do for her—whether the issue is financial help, heroic medical measures, assisted suicide, or emotional support. It's fine to say, "I don't know," if that's an honest response. It's not fine to lie and falsify facts about issues that matter to her.

Instead of offering false assurances, address the nursing home issue frankly. Ask your mother what upsets her most about a nursing home (now more frequently called a health care center). How many nursing homes has she actually visited? Would she like to visit one with you? Did she have a parent or other relative in a nursing home, and, if so, how did that go?

How mad will she be at you if she ends up in a nursing home? Will she stop speaking to you? Will she stop loving you? Would she ever forgive you? How does she imagine that life in a nursing home would change her relationship with you, including the frequency of visits?

> Lies erode trust. Your mother has the right to consider her future based on facts, no matter how difficult.

Don't bombard her with these questions, but try instead to talk with her, and other family members (you need them), over time. Don't dwell on the negative and don't lapse into lies. Be courageous. When we say, "I can't tell my mother because it will cause her too much pain," we may really mean that we ourselves don't want to deal with her pain and anger—or our own.

What matters most is that you and other family members stay connected to your mother, wherever she resides. Your mother will ultimately gather her resources to deal with her situation. She will do less well if family members try to protect her by deceiving her, or if they try to protect themselves by distancing from her.

Keeping a Secret

Dear Harriet:

A week ago, my older sister, Jan, who lives in another state, called to tell me her life is falling apart. Her husband has announced that he plans to leave her, and she just lost her job. She swore me to secrecy because she thinks our mother can't handle such bad news. I see our mother every day and we are very close. Jan's secret is constantly on my mind. I feel I'm ready to burst. I also think my mother should know that Jan is terribly depressed. But if I tell my mother, Jan will be furious and never confide in me again. Is Jan right to put me in this bind? Help!

Dear Reader:

Your dilemma is one that we all will struggle with at one time or another in family life. When a sister or brother tells us to keep something confidential, is it *always* our responsibility to do so? And at what cost?

It's not a simple matter of right and wrong. Jan has the right to ask you to keep information confidential. You have the right to decide that it is too big a secret to keep. And Jan has the right to be angry in response. One person's right to be angry doesn't mean that the other person is wrong.

The challenge is this: How can you make the most responsible and thoughtful decision possible—one that takes into account your responsibility to your sister, your mother, and yourself?

A good place to begin is to share your predicament with Jan in a letter or phone call. For example:

Jan, I've been thinking a lot about you, and I realize I'm having trouble keeping quiet about your problems. When I'm keeping such an important secret from Mom, my relationship with her is strained and uncomfortable. I try to act as if nothing is happening, but when we're together I end up feeling tense. Also, I love you and want to be helpful, but I don't feel I can be helpful enough all by myself. I wish the entire family, including Mom, knew about your situation so we could all be in your corner—and not just me alone.

At the same time, it's not my business to tell Mom what's going on with you or to share something important about your life that you've asked me not to share. This doesn't feel right to me, either.

So it's a big dilemma for me, and I haven't been able to get clear about it. I'd really like to hear your thoughts about this.

Lay out the dilemma without blaming Jan or telling her what to do. Your sister may then provide you with new information. Jan might say that she's gathering her courage to tell your mother herself, and she needs more time. You may decide you can live with that. Or she might tell you that she has no plans to tell your mother, and if you do, she will never speak to you again.

If you do breach Jan's confidence, understand that she's going to be angry, and if you were in her shoes, you'd probably feel the same. Tell Jan that in the future you want to be out of the confidant business when it comes to keeping such serious news from your mother. Let her know it's too difficult for you.

Here's some general advice about secret-keeping between siblings:

Each generation shares private communications, which is fine. Siblings share confidences that are not for parents' ears, and parents do the same.

It's a good idea to consider getting out of the secret-keeping business, however, when keeping secrets occurs at the expense of another important relationship—in this case, yours with your mother. It's also a problem when secrets cross generations. (Mom says, "Don't tell Dad!")

Most important, if your sister is considering some self-injurious act—perhaps even suicide—no room exists for family secrets. The most helpful thing in such a case is to open up the lines of communication and for all family members to be direct about their concerns. Jan, of course, may not be at risk. You say she is "terribly depressed"—but who wouldn't be in her situation? Have you asked Jan if things have hit her so hard that she's thought about hurting herself?

> Your sister has the right to ask you to keep information confidential. You have a right to decide when a secret is too big to keep.

Consider whether some of the pressure you are feeling may reflect an overly anxious response to Jan's struggle, particularly if you lack confidence in your sister's competence to manage her own problems and pain. But if you are still "ready to burst" in your mother's presence, it may simply be too weighty a secret to keep.

As for the notion that "Mother can't handle it"—I would challenge your sister on that one. Family members are often protected from information on the grounds that they are weak, vulnerable, or otherwise can't handle it. In most cases they handle it just fine.

My Mother Is Driving Me Crazy

Dear Harriet:

My widowed mother, Ida, is the most selfish, demand-ing, and manipulative woman in the world. She insists that I do her grocery shopping the day she decides she needs something. She invites herself to spend every holiday with my husband and me, including New Year's Eve, and she won't take no for an answer. If she doesn't get her way, she cries, gets cold as ice, or reminds us she may not be around for the next holiday. We go along in the end or we pay a price. Aren't her demands unreasonable? How can I convince her to get some psychological help?

Dear Reader:

Your mother may not want help, nor does she neces-sarily have a problem. After all, she is able to identify her wishes and make requests on her own behalf. She's even able to get her way. The problem is yours. You give in to Ida's demands and then blame her for being so difficult.

Of course, having a problem is not the same as being the problem. Nor does it imply that you are wrong, or to blame, or the cause of your dilemma. It's simply to say that you're dissatisfied with your situation, and if you don't do something about it, no one else will.

Get clear about who is responsible for what. Ida can't make you feel guilty, nor is it in her power to manipulate you. She can only try. You're responsible for your own feel-ings, guilt included, and for making decisions about what you will and will not do. If Ida, in response, gets angry or feels depressed, it's her job to learn how to manage those feelings.

Are Ida's demands unreasonable? If we were to ask ten different people "How much should a widowed mother ask of her child?" or "How much should a grown daughter give?" we might get ten different answers, depending on each respondent's age, religion, sibling position, socioeconomic class, and ethnic background. There's no right or wrong answer.

Clarify your values and stand behind them with dignity and firmness—while respecting your mother's right to think and feel differently. Your dilemma does not stem from a lack of assertiveness but, more likely, from a lack of inner clarity. Like most women, you may be struggling to sort out some very difficult issues: What is my responsibility to myself, and what is my responsibility to my mother? When am I being selfish, and when am I being true to my own wants and priorities? How much can I do or give without feeling resentful and depressed? Which is worse: to say yes and feel resentful or say no and feel guilty?

> If you give in to your mother's demands and then blame her for being so difficult, the problem is yours.

Identify one or two small areas where you can test the waters by saying no, and then stand firmly behind your decision when Ida begins her guilt-inducing maneuvers. Don't expect your mother to like the changes you make. Relationships don't work that way.

When we introduce new steps to an old dance, we can count on the other person to make a countermove in an attempt to reinstate the status quo. If you decide, for example, to tell Ida that you and your husband want to spend New Year's Eve alone together, prepare for her strong reaction to the news.

If Ida becomes critical ("How can you be so selfish?"), don't become critical in return. Simply restate your position ("Well, maybe it's selfish of me, but it's just real important to me to be alone with Bob"). If she tries to debate the issue ("You and Bob can be together every night of the year. What's so sacred about this one?"), don't become defensive or argue back. Instead show her you empathize with her reaction ("I'm sorry that I'm causing you hurt, Mom. I'm aware that being with us on New Year's Eve means a lot to you").

It's normal for Ida to continue to test you over time to see if you really mean it. She may act bitter or depressed. She may make overt or disguised threats to sever your relationship entirely. Your task is to establish a position around an issue (begin with a small one) and then to stand behind it. Most important, you should do your best to stay in warm emotional contact with Ida without getting intense or becoming reactive to her provocative behavior.

If you can meet this challenge over time, Ida will calm down and your relationship will improve. You may even find yourself navigating all your relationships with greater clarity and calm.

The Power of the Unconscious

Dear Harriet:

Ever since my thirtieth birthday I've been feeling depressed. My mother was thirty-three when she died. A friend thinks my depression is an "anniversary reaction" to my mom's death. I'm not sure what this means.

Dear Reader:

Anniversary dates exert a powerful influence on our emotional functioning. It's as if the unconscious remembers and reacts when we, or our children, reach a particularly loaded age.

Here are a few examples of typical anniversary reactions.

- When Lucia's son turned eight, Lucia became preoccupied with his well-being and anxious about her own health. Lucia's sister had been diagnosed with a brain tumor at age eight.

- Ivan began making unwise business decisions at age thirty-two. That was the age when his dad went bankrupt and lost his business.

- Rochelle's daughter was five years old when Rochelle began an affair with her boss. When Rochelle was her daughter's age, her parents separated and later divorced.

Anniversary dates create an anxious emotional field in family life. We may fail to connect a particular problem (say, an infidelity) with an anniversary date, or we may not even "know" the important dates in our family history. Learning the key dates of pivotal events in our family history provides us with a larger context in which to understand our behavior. We can begin to think about the real sources of the anxiety that affects us at a particular time, rather than acting out or acting up in nonproductive ways.

> The anniversary of a loss can create a crisis, but it can also be an opportunity to rework old issues and move forward.

As for your depression, it's normal for you to experience buried feelings surrounding the loss of your mom at this time. Anniversary dates may create crises, but they also present an opportunity to rework unresolved issues and move forward. Consider, too, what other meanings turning thirty might have for you. The decade birthdays are always big milestones in our lives.

Is It Weird to Plan Your Own Funeral?

Dear Harriet:

I'm having trouble with my parents, who are almost ninety and in failing health. My mother is planning every last detail of her funeral, including what I should wear. My father wants his body to go to a medical center, and he opposes having a funeral or ritual of any sort. I believe funerals are for the living, and I want to plan a traditional burial service for both of them. The more I argue with them, the more stubborn they become. What would you do in my shoes?

Dear Reader:

Your parents, at almost ninety, have earned the right to be stubborn. How wonderful that they're able to consider their impending deaths and make their wishes known! It makes sense that your mom and dad want their deaths to reflect their tastes and the values they live by or aspire to. I admire their plucky and independent spirits.

I would honor my parents' requests as much as possible. I hope my children would do the same for me. But I wouldn't make any promises I might not keep. If my dad asked me to spread his ashes in seventeen cities, I would tell him it's just not feasible. I'd follow my parents' wishes, but I would also define my own limits ("No, Mom, I'm *not* going to wear my yellow dress to the service"; "Sorry, but I *am* planning to call Aunt Mary when you die, because I would feel too uncomfortable excluding her").

Your father's plan to donate his body to science deserves respect, as does your need to ritualize and mark his death. Perhaps you can reassure your dad that there will be no formal funeral service for him. You may, however, create a service or ritual for yourself—to honor, reflect, and remember his life and to move on with yours. Be inventive in creating a ritual that takes into consideration the individuals you both are.

What bothers you about your mother's wish to control her funeral? Women and the elderly have far too little con-

> If your father wants you to spread
> his ashes in seventeen cities, you can tell
> him it's just not feasible.

trol over what happens to them while they're alive, and this is a chance for you to respect your mother's wishes without judgment or condescension. You can also gather some humor and appreciation for these strong-willed folks. Maybe it's easier for you to fight with your parents than to feel sad about their impending death, but consider what you can do differently to allow for a broader range of feelings and conversation during this final phase of their lives.

6

≋

Then Comes Marriage

Introduction

Sharpen your pencil and prepare to take Harriet Lerner's "Good Marriage Test."

Imagine that a beneficent goddess descends from on high and decrees that every married couple in America must live separately for one year. Each couple must set up two new households, say, about twenty minutes apart from each other. You and your spouse can visit, but not more than once a week. After a year apart, all parties will make a fresh decision about their marital status.

In her ultimate generosity and goodwill, the goddess removes all economic and practical worries for each spouse, forevermore. You're assured interesting, well-paid work or career training, a nice place to live, and, say, half a million dollars to invest. The goddess offers her own hand-maidens to provide all the worry-free child care either parent ever needs.

You can now easily pay for whatever services your spouse has provided, like cooking, fixing the stereo, shopping, or figuring your taxes. If you're ever unable to function independently, be it from a broken arm or a more seri-

214 ≋ Life Preservers

ous health problem, all levels of quality care are automatically provided. Financially speaking, you're set for life.

Our omniscient goddess removes all the negative emotions that hold women in place—like fear ("If I get sick, who'll take care of me?") or guilt ("He'd be devastated if I left him") or self-doubt ("I'd be too scared to live alone") or worry about children (they'll do fine in one household or two). She also makes sure that no one will get mad at you, or disapprove, or suffer, whatever life you choose.

Our goddess, being playful, throws in a final trick. All marriages legally dissolve. So if you want to be married to your current partner when the year is up, you have to go down to the marriage license bureau and fill out the appropriate forms.

Consider, now, that your year apart is almost up. Some of you will have made your decision the day you were set up in your terrific new place. For these folks, the year has not been so much an experiment as a liberation. The rest of you have had twelve months to get to know yourself and your spouse better, under new conditions of equality and in the absence of guilt and fear.

As you ponder your decision, you become curious about what other American women will choose to do. The goddess, who sees the future as well as the back of her hand, wants you to know exactly how things will fall out, so she gives you the fact sheet on the next page to review before you make your final decision.

Fact Sheet
Postseparation Marital Demographics

Category 1 (Remarry for Right Reasons)

Seventeen (17) percent of all American women will choose to remarry the same guy. Of these couples, half get back under the same roof and half prefer the separate living arrangement. Women in this category remarry for sensible reasons, like love, comfort, desire, relaxation, nurturance, good sex, good conversation, good silence, and just feeling better when they're around each other.

Category 2 (Remarry for Wrong Reasons)

Fourteen (14) percent of all American women remarry because of ingrained unspecified fears that the goddess, even in her omnipotent wisdom, forgot to remove from the female psyche. Even a goddess couldn't guess how thoroughly such fears are conditioned and how deeply they lurk.

Category 3 (Stay Single and Stay Friends)

Thirty-six (36) percent of all women don't remarry or resume an exclusive partnership. But they consider their ex-husbands to be among their best friends. Occasionally, they may be lovers.

Category 4 (Stay Single and Don't Really Like the Guy So Much)

Thirty-three (33) percent of all women don't remarry and don't think to call their ex-husbands if they want company for dinner or a movie or just someone to hang out with.

Why does the wise goddess want you to contemplate these statistics *before* you make your final decision? She understands that women, being only human, will want to know what most women do and will want to be part of the group that accrues status, approval, and privilege. Historically speaking, this has meant marriage. But this fact sheet shows that married women will now be a minority in American society—an alternative lifestyle, if you will. Never again will single women feel "one down" in any way. The experiment has created a total equality of status for all sorts of living arrangements—straight, gay, and some not yet even imagined. OK, so the year is up, you have a good house, a good job, good friends, good financial security. What category do you fall into?

My point isn't really to have you rate yourself (goddess only knows we do enough of that). Nor do I wish to reduce the complex institution of marriage to a simple how-much-do-you-genuinely-like-this-guy scale. Nor do I mean to create a higher power who will make us all terribly middle-class and consumer/comfort oriented.

But I do want to give you a new slant on an old institution. Marriage would look oh so very different if it were freely chosen, one of many celebrated and socially rewarded alternatives, by two economically equal partners who always had the choice to live well without each other but preferred not to.

Under these hypothetical conditions, I think fewer women would marry to begin with, and those who did would have more viable, more mutually enhancing relationships. Paradoxically, there is something about the hidden coercive nature of marriage and its long legacy of economic and social inequality that has everything to do with why it so often doesn't go well.

I recently attended a professional workshop presented by family therapist Betty Carter, a renowned expert on marriage, divorce, and stepfamilies. She ran the familiar statistics by us—a divorce rate for first marriages that jiggles between 49 and 50 percent and a significantly higher divorce rate for second marriages (about 64 percent)—then raised the following question, "If an institution slates 50 percent of its people for failure—as the institution of marriage does—what's wrong with the *institution*? What is it about this thing called marriage that produces a 50 percent no-go rate?"

It's one of those obvious questions that people don't tend to "see." If any *other* social institution had a 50 percent failure rate, Carter noted, we'd have to reexamine the institution itself, not just the individuals who dropped out of it, to say nothing of those who stayed in and felt unhappy. Yet when people divorce, they blame themselves, or their spouse, rather than questioning the roles and rules of marriage today—and the social inequities and work demands affecting marriage from the larger culture. It's as if each single divorce statistic represents someone's very own personal failure.

Today, we're nothing short of pioneers. Because heterosexual marriage is only one form of pairing in a world that is rich with possibilities for intimacy and connection, some of us are creating joyful lives that don't include marriage or men. Others are struggling to make marriage work and to form a more equal and mutually growth-enhancing partnership.

It's a tall order or, more accurately, a lifelong challenge. Being a pioneer is never easy. But when it comes to women and marriage, there are no "good old days" to head back to, even if we could.

My Husband Betrayed Me

Dear Harriet:

A month ago I discovered that my husband, Max, was having an affair. When I confronted him, he immediately stopped seeing the woman. Part of me is obsessed with the betrayal, but I haven't questioned him further, because we decided to put it behind us. I haven't confided in anyone. My problem is that I still feel devastated. I told Max that if he is ever unfaithful to me again, I'm out the door with the kids and filing for divorce the next day. He swears that it will never happen again, but how can I trust him to keep his promise?

Dear Reader:

When you and Max married, you took an oath to forsake all others. However, many husbands and wives don't keep this promise. Statistics suggest a very high incidence of extramarital affairs; they are not terrible aberrations that only happen in unhappy marriages. For any number of reasons, we are just not as monogamous as we would like to be.

The false idea that we are an entirely monogamous species encourages denial ("My husband is never attracted to other women"), isolation and shame ("I wouldn't want anyone to know that my husband betrayed me"), and exaggerated feelings of personal failure ("What was wrong with me that he needed to go outside the relationship?"). As a result, many people, like yourself, are hesitant to talk about extramarital affairs.

If you're truly committed to the marriage and to

rebuilding lost trust, reconsider your ultimatum to rush out the door if you find out about another transgression. The message this sends to Max is *"Don't dare tell me if you act on—or even experience—another temptation,"* and such a stance may actually invite deception, making future affairs more likely.

Instead, you might ask Max to make a commitment to honesty—not only about his present and future sexual attractions, but about all of the emotional issues affecting your relationship. Future temptations may well arise for either of you, and they are most likely to be acted upon if they can't be addressed openly in the marriage or even mentioned. As Peggy Vaughn notes in her book, *The Monogamy Myth*, trust in marriage evolves only from a true knowledge of our partner and of ourself and a mutual commitment to sharing and self-disclosure.

> We need to acknowledge openly that strong attractions—and affairs—can occur in even the best of marriages.

In line with the goal of enhancing communication and closeness, consider learning more about Max's affair. It will be painful for you to question him about the details, but you will probably do better with facts than with fantasies and fears. If you gradually ask Max the questions you are ready to hear answers to, he may refine and expand on the truths he can tell you. Try not to punish him for his honesty, even when the truth is difficult to hear.

Express your desire to talk with Max about attractions *before* they are acted upon—and to hear the facts directly from him if he does have sex with another woman. You might say, "Although it would be devastating to hear the truth from you, I would be more able to stay in the marriage at least long enough to work with you to get some clarity about it, so we could then make a thoughtful decision about where to go from there. Because if I discovered that you were having an affair and lying to me about it, our marriage would be in far greater jeopardy."

Consider sharing your experience with people you trust. Maintaining secrecy only enhances feelings of shame, encourages you to focus narrowly on Max's transgression, and blocks you from the support you deserve. Certain friends or family may respond in unhelpful ways; by blaming you or your husband, putting down your marriage, giving unsolicited advice, over- or underreacting, or telling you that you must leave (or must never leave) Max.

Let people know precisely what you do and don't find helpful and supportive. For example, if you want a friend to listen to your feelings and share her experiences, let her know. If you want her to distract you on a particular day, tell her so.

Marital counseling can help you and Max sort out the emotional issues and events that may have contributed to the affair. But we need to acknowledge openly with our spouse that strong attractions—and affairs—can occur in even the best of marriages. Paradoxically, monogamy becomes more attainable when we recognize that we can't guarantee it or take it on faith. Work to establish honesty and communication in your marriage, which is the only foundation on which trust can be built.

Premenstrual Syndrome or Premenstrual Sanity?

Dear Harriet:

During the week before my period starts I become extremely irritable toward my husband, Eddie. I even throw temper tantrums about the fact that he is sloppy and never cleans up after himself. Eddie is convinced I suffer from severe PMS because I'm pleasant the other three weeks of the month. He also says that my aggressive outbursts are proof that women's hormones are unstable and we can't function under stress. I know his views are dated, but it's hard to argue when PMS makes me "not myself" and ultimately proves his point.

Dear Reader:

Hormonal changes associated with the menstrual cycle may, indeed, heighten your emotional intensity and make you feel "not yourself." But these changes may also make you "more yourself," if you can recognize and voice complaints at this time. The term *premenstrual sanity* is a fitting diagnostic label for women who use premenstrual changes as an opportunity to tell a spouse—or themselves—what they otherwise don't dare to.

Women often disqualify their own legitimate anger by venting it in a manner that allows others to write them off as irrational, hysterical, infantile, or, in your case, "at-that-time-of-the-month." Respect your outbursts as a signal that something is not right, and consider how you really feel about Eddie's unwillingness to clean up after himself.

How do you imagine Eddie would respond if you approached him calmly (say, over the course of your three "good" weeks in the month) and asked him to pull his weight in the housework department? If you shared distress about his behavior—and he didn't change over time—what would that say about his regard for you? Do you feel heard in your marriage, on this and other important issues?

> We disqualify our own legitimate anger when we allow others to write us off as irrational or, in your case, "at-that-time-of-the-month."

As for raging female hormones, let's face it: does Eddie stay off the streets at night because he fears attacks from uncontrolled, irrational women in the throes of premenstrual syndrome? Probably not. Women stay home at night because they fear the irrational behavior of men. From the subway station or dark alley to our nation's capital, it is specifically male behavior that should merit attention and concern.

The research on hormones and aggression suggests we would do well to shift our primary attention from progesterone to testosterone. High testosterone in men has been linked to antisocial behavior such as delinquency and substance abuse, but that hasn't made headlines. Social psychologist Carol Tavris asks why we have a syndrome called PMS but not one called HTS—hypertestosterone syndrome.

Ultimately though, as Tavris notes in her book *The Mismeasure of Woman*, hormones alone can't "make" men or women engage in unsavory behaviors, or virtuous ones, for that matter. Just as it's unlikely that Eddie's hormones prevent him from picking up his socks, it's equally unlikely that your hormones force you to blow up at him. Nothing is "just hormonal" or "just in our head." Many forces combine to make overreacting and underreacting a predictable part of human emotional life, along with rudeness, grumpiness, and every variety of inconsiderate behavior.

This is not to minimize the symptoms you experience before your period. We should all educate ourselves about hormone shifts associated with menstruation, pregnancy, and menopause so that we can avoid viewing ourselves as neurotic complainers. But the "diseasing" of women's natural hormonal and reproductive cycles has a very long history. We need to ask why there has been *so much* focus on the "problematic nature" of female reproductive cycles and *so little* focus on the real health issues that affect our lives.

My Husband Is Jealous of
My Therapist

Dear Harriet:

I started therapy five weeks ago and my husband, Jack, really wants to know what I talk about in my sessions. I have refused to tell him anything because I feel that what goes on between me and my therapist is private. Now Jack has begun to criticize my therapist even though he has never met him. My therapist, who is a very warm and caring doctor, thinks my husband is feeling threatened because I am forming a close relationship with another man. Do you agree?

Dear Reader:

Sure. It's normal for one spouse to feel threatened when the other enters therapy. Jack's anxiety may also reflect his fears that therapy will threaten your marriage, cause conflict, or put distance between the two of you. His fears may or may not be realistic.

Marriage is a primary relationship in which each partner typically expects to be placed first by the other. If you are somehow communicating to Jack that you have a "special" relationship with your doctor, with whom you share your most intimate thoughts and feelings, then why shouldn't Jack be jealous?

Jack may also have his own concerns that lead him to be particularly sensitive to feeling like the outsider in this triangle. But therapy does sometimes function at the expense of one spouse. Jack's feeling of being excluded may be reinforced if you are talking *about* him and not *with* him about whatever troubles you. And if you fail to provide your husband with some clear facts about your treatment—not so much the specifics, but what a session is like and what you get out of it—his anxiety and fantasies about what goes on there will only multiply.

> It's normal for one spouse to feel threatened when the other enters therapy.

Do you have the right to complete privacy in your work with your therapist? Of course you do. You're under no obligation to tell your husband everything you think and feel. But privacy is not the same as secrecy or emotional distance.

My advice is to fill Jack in a bit, while respecting your own feelings with regard to what you're not ready to share. It really is possible to do both. Work on changing your part in the current marital dance in which Jack pursues you for information and you refuse to disclose.

I'm Monogamous, He Isn't

Dear Harriet:

I have been in emotional pain throughout my five-year marriage. My husband, Barnett, has never been able to stay out of other women's beds. He claims that monogamy isn't natural for human beings and that we are brainwashed into believing it is. I disagree, and think this is his problem, not mine. What do you think?

Dear Reader:

Whether monogamy is or isn't a natural state for all humans, your husband believes it's not natural for him, and that's what matters. It makes little difference whether Barnett's behavior is driven by his hormones, his toilet training, or the phases of the moon. What matters is that he rejects monogamy and you are in pain.

From this perspective, *you* have the problem. This is not to imply that you are misguided or wrong. It is only to say that you are the one unhappy with the current situation, and if you don't take some action on your own behalf, no one else will do it for you. You may decide that you don't like Barnett's behavior but that you will live with it because you don't want to end the marriage. Or, alterna-

> It makes no difference whether your husband's affairs are driven by his hormones, his toilet training, or the phases of the moon. What matters is that you are in pain.

tively, you may one day tell Barnett that you can't cope with his behavior and if he continues to sleep with other women, you will leave him. Either way, it's your job to make a decision that you can accept, live with, and follow through on.

People often claim that a particular behavior is "natural" or "biological" when they don't want to change it. But the fact that humans are naturally predisposed to behave one way or another tells us very little about whether a particular behavior is right or moral or good for us. Nor is biology necessarily immutable. The fact that something is part of our biological nature doesn't mean it's as fixed as the stars. It's sometimes easier to modify biological tendencies than to alter deeply entrenched learned patterns.

Is monogamy good for every human? It depends on whom you ask. Feminist scholar Sonia Johnson, for example, argues that monogamy is "the red herring of numbers that focuses us on how many lovers we are taking naked to bed instead of what condition our souls are in and what is in our hearts as we lie with them." Others view monogamy in marriage as sacred.

The challenge for you is to clarify *your* values and beliefs. If your words say one thing ("I can't live with this") and your actions say another (you continue to live with it), actions speak louder. Take all the time you need to think about your options and formulate a plan. Share your dilemma with others and gather their perspectives. But remember that no one else can know for certain what is best for you.

Don't spin your wheels with Barnett, arguing about who's right or debating the nature-versus-nurture controversy. Do keep telling him how much pain you are in. If and when Barnett is faced with the actual choice of losing you or stopping his affairs, you will have a clearer picture of his priorities and his motivation to curb his "natural" ways.

I'm Not Mrs. Smith!

Dear Harriet:

When I married my husband last month, he didn't take my name and I didn't take his. But his mother introduces us as "the Smiths" and writes letters to "Mr. and Mrs. Smith." I've corrected her twice, but she is determined to "forget." Why is it such a big deal that I've kept my maiden name? Isn't it my husband's job to confront his mother about this?

Dear Reader:

For starters, I suggest that we drop the outdated term *maiden name* from our vocabulary. Refer instead to *birth name, family-of-origin name,* or simply, *name.* Surely, the surname that we were born and raised with no longer relates to our status as maidens.

The subject of names in marriage is a loaded issue because it reflects a woman's subordinate position in our cultures. You couldn't convince members of the dominant group (i.e., men) that they should take their spouse's name in marriage any more than you could convince them that words like *womankind, she,* and *chairwoman* truly include them. An individual woman may not feel compromised by taking her husband's name. But when such a tradition is assumed and assigned by gender, it reflects institutionalized inequality.

By retaining your surname, you're challenging a tradition of male dominance that has deep roots in history and culture. It's natural that you will be tested many times by family members and others to see if you will stand firmly behind your decision. Correcting people over and over—your mother-in-law, your neighbors, the IRS—is simply part of being a pioneer. And it's something that you should consider your job, not your husband's. Brace yourself to sound like a broken record, if necessary.

> You couldn't convince men to take their spouse's name in marriage any more than you could convince them that the words *she* and *chairwoman* truly include them.

Your mother-in-law's "forgetfulness" may reflect other issues as well. Has her son chosen a wife whose values and beliefs differ markedly from her own? If so, she may unconsciously experience his choice as a rejection, a threat, a betrayal, or a potential loss. But if they find it hard to talk together about sensitive subjects, the emotions may be detoured toward you.

For this reason, be light, low-keyed, and even humorous in correcting your mother-in-law about your name. If you become critical or intense, you may, like a lightning rod, protect your husband by absorbing the negative emotion from his family. Try correcting your mother-in-law by teasing her affectionately rather than by confronting her.

Remember that change is always accompanied by anxiety. If you consider the enormity of the changes women have made in the last several decades, your mother-in-law's resistance will seem less like a personal affront. When things are calm and comfortable between the two of you, try to talk with her directly about her reactions to your decision to keep your name. Listen without getting defensive. Respect her right to think and feel differently.

And if you think this situation is difficult, ask yourself how you will solve the naming problem when the first baby arrives? This is when our bedrock-feminist values are really put to the test!

My Husband Left Me for a Man

Dear Harriet:

After twenty years of marriage, my husband, Scott, suddenly packed his bags and left me for a rich male lover. His parting note said that he had discovered his "real self" and that he had to act on his "true feelings." My husband was my entire life, and I thought we had a perfect and problem-free marriage. Until he left, I had no hint he was gay. Two months have passed since our divorce and I'm still enraged, humiliated, and miserable. I feel betrayed, my femininity destroyed.

Dear Reader:

It is devastating to be left. You have experienced a profoundly traumatic loss, from which it will understandably take you a long time to recover. The most important task you have right now is to take good care of yourself. Above all, you should not be isolated in your grief.

When Scott walked out, you lost more than your most significant relationship. You also lost your identity and self-regard, as well as your sense of history, continuity, and meaning. Scott's decision to leave you, and to come out as gay, forces you to revise both your understanding of the past and your pictures of the future. It is normal to feel crushed and overwhelmed.

The end of your marriage may be particularly confusing and painful because, clearly, you and Scott were not talking about marital problems as they occurred. Scott did not share his feelings of dissatisfaction, nor did he openly discuss his struggle with his sexual orientation. Neither of you addressed—or perhaps even recognized—the emotional distance between you. If the two of you had been able to talk more openly, you might feel on more solid ground now. A sudden loss is more devastating and disorienting than one that we can see coming, try to understand, and plan for.

Further contributing to your pain is the perceived insult of Scott desiring a man over you. But neither Scott's decision to leave you nor your earlier choice of him as a marriage partner has anything to do with your femininity. You have no way of knowing, unless Scott tells you, whether he has always struggled with being gay or whether he discovered this aspect of himself more recently. Some people can, and do, change their sexual orientation later in life, but more frequently they deny their homosexuality from

> When your husband left you for a man, it forced you to revise both your understanding of the past and your pictures of the future.

the start (even to themselves) and try to adapt to marriage. Unfortunately, as long as we continue to stigmatize and disregard homosexual pairings, individuals will attempt to suppress their real feelings, and the painful reality you've encountered will be all too common.

Here are a few suggestions for getting through this difficult time:

Let people know how they can best support you. If you want a friend to listen to you and unconditionally accept whatever you are feeling, let her know.

If you haven't done so already, get an AIDS test now—and then again in six months. Even if Scott denies ever having had sex outside your marriage, you owe it to yourself to be sure you haven't been exposed. This is true whether you suspect your husband has been unfaithful with another man or another woman.

Work on a plan that will allow you to live your life as well as possible. How can you strengthen your connections to family and friends? What talents, abilities, and interests would you like to develop over the next five years? What actions are you taking to ensure your own economic viability? Currently, it may take all your energy just to get through the day. In time, though, you will be able to consider the future.

When you are feeling calmer and less vulnerable, consider talking to Scott about your marriage and when he realized he was gay. It's understandable if you don't want to speak to him now, since it's not useful for anyone to try to process painful emotional issues when we're feeling enraged or otherwise emotionally intense. The situation may feel different, however, in six months or two years.

No marriage is "perfect and problem-free," as you believed yours to be, and it won't help you to move on if you idealize the past. Of course, Scott's current lifestyle doesn't invalidate the good things you shared together, either. To obtain a more accurate and balanced picture of your life together, you and Scott both need to understand each other's perspective. How do each of you think your marriage changed over time? What role did you both play in blocking open conversation about problems and complaints? Sexuality aside, what were the strengths and shortcomings of your marriage? What shifts in closeness and distance did each of you experience over the years?

It's painful to search out the facts, but it's even harder in the long run to obsess over unknowns or flounder around in your imagination. Having a more objective picture of your respective contributions to your marital problems will ultimately strengthen you. Of course, all this may be possible only later, when you feel stronger and less overwhelmed.

When we put all our eggs in the basket of one relationship, we risk losing everything when that relationship ends. When marriage is our "entire life," it becomes too threatening to notice marital problems, and it becomes equally difficult for the other person to address them directly with us. Losing oneself in marriage is what our culture encourages; it is not a reflection of personal failure.

Remember that you and Scott were married for two decades and that you have been divorced for only two months. You have years ahead of you to make sense out of what has happened and to get your life back on course.

I'm White, He's Black

Dear Harriet:

Last month I married the most perfect man in the world, Jesse, who happens to be African-American. My Irish Catholic, widowed mother didn't go to the wedding and now refuses to allow Jesse into her home. I'm furious, but I'm also scared of losing her. I keep trying to convince her that color makes no difference at all and that people are all the same, but it's like talking to a block of ice. How can I make her accept him?

Dear Reader:

You've heard this before: you can't "make" your mother do anything. It's impossible to change another person's thoughts and feelings, and the more you try, the more likely your mother will dig in her heels. Your mother may never accept Jesse.

I question your assumption that "color makes no difference." Of course color makes a difference. Your white, Irish Catholic mother has a different legacy and heritage from your African-American husband. Of equal value and worth, yes. The same, no.

Your mother is not alone in her feelings. Friends and business associates may also respond negatively to your marriage. We all absorb the values of our racist society. Truly learning to value differences requires a very high level of maturity as well as life experience. Most people feel threatened by differences and live narrowly circumscribed lives.

Rather than trying to convince your mother that Jesse is "the same," become a good listener and questioner. To have any kind of relationship with your mother, you need to have some understanding of her intense reaction. You might ask her without judgment or anger: "Mom, what disturbs you most about my marrying a black man?" "What is your biggest fear or worry about it?" "How would Dad react if he were alive today?" "What about your mother and father?" "Who else in the family do you think is having a hard time with my choice?" "Which of our relatives do you think might have less of a problem accepting Jesse?" "How did your own parents feel about your choice of a husband?"

Questioning can help you view your mother's reactions through a wider lens and across generations. Such questions can also help you prepare for the opposition to your marriage that you will encounter from other people. It will also teach you more about your heritage How much do you know about how differences have been managed in your extended family? Who else has married out of the family's religion or ethnic group? Have your parents ever been excluded because of being Irish Catholic? The hot issues of one generation get passed down to the next.

> Of course race makes a difference.

To set the stage for asking questions, you might begin by sharing some of your *own* concerns, too ("Sometimes I worry that other African-Americans will see Jesse as a traitor for marrying me"). It will not be easy, but give it a try. Such sharing will help to loosen the polarized positions in which you and your mother are now stuck. Currently, it is as if *all* the worry is in your mother and *all* the positive feelings are in you. Under stress, family members tend to move into polarized positions that block them from owning the more complex and mixed feelings that we all have. No wonder you're deadlocked.

Most important of all, keep in mind that the challenge you face now is part of a long-term process that will take place slowly over many years, perhaps a lifetime. Trust that you will have many opportunities to clarify where you stand with your mother, ideally without trying to change her or becoming cut off from her.

For example, your mother might continue not to allow Jesse into her house. Your position might be that you don't like her decision or agree with it, but you can live with it ("It's very painful to me, Mother, that Jesse isn't welcome in your home, because I really love you both. But it would be even more painful to me to lose my relationship with you, so I'll continue to drop by without him").

In another circumstance, you may decide that you can't go along with your mother's dictates ("Mother, I'm sorry but I'm not able to accept your insistence that I not bring Jesse to Uncle John's funeral. Jesse is my husband and I want him by my side at this time. I regret any pain this may cause you, but we will be at the church together").

If you can clarify your values calmly and respectfully without trying to convince your mother to see things your way, all three of you will have the best chance of becoming more connected over time. Also, keep the lines of communication open between you and Jesse about the joys and hardships you anticipate in your marriage. Share both sides with family members as openly as you can.

Last but not least, remember that a wedding is a major event in the life cycle of any family. Weddings stir up intense emotions, particularly if there is a significant loss (in this case, your dad) in the background. Your recent marriage might have evoked strong feelings in family members (yourself included) even if you had chosen a partner with impeccable Irish Catholic credentials. And the more you focus on your mother's reactions, the less in touch you will be with your own.

P.S. There is no perfect man (or woman) of any color.

I Love the Guy,
but the Sex Is Terrible

Dear Harriet:

I was a virgin when I married almost one year ago. Since then, sex has been an ordeal. My husband, Neil, pays no attention to trying to arouse me and will only have intercourse with me in the one sexual position he likes. His idea of foreplay is to rub his erect penis against my hip to let me know he's ready. I've tried a few times to discuss how unsatisfied I feel, and I've even left him notes, but I haven't gotten anywhere. I love him, but I feel so desperate I'm thinking about leaving him.

Dear Reader:

For the moment, forget about good sex and concentrate on good conversation. Pick a calm time when you are not in bed and tell Neil that you want to talk. Have as your goal the wish to know him better as a person and a sexual human being. The challenge for you is to find new ways to talk to him about your feelings and to be heard.

Over time begin to ask Neil specific questions: What's his experience making love to you? Is this the only way he's ever had sex? Does he think there's a problem? Can he tell you something about his family or sexual history that would help you to understand his behavior? Does it matter to him that you feel unsatisfied and desperate? Why is he failing to consider you?

The value of opening up a conversation with Neil is not simply to fix this one problem or to get him to expand his currently unimaginative sexual repertoire. Nor do you need to have a marathon session in which you cover everything. Rather, I'm suggesting that you test Neil's capacity, as well as your own, to discuss difficult issues over time, and to remain emotionally present with each other when differences emerge.

> If the problem is so serious that you're considering divorce, tell this to your husband as often as it takes to make sure he gets it.

The sexual problem you describe is certainly serious, and your feeling of desperation is understandable, but don't let it obscure all your other relationship issues. Sex aside, is Neil someone who pays attention to your needs? Is he responsive when you voice a desire or complaint? How well are you and Neil able to talk about your differences and find solutions that take into account both of your needs?

Work on finding and asserting your own voice both within and outside the relationship. Get clear about what you expect from marriage in order to stay in it, and what you will tolerate. Neil's sexual behavior won't change if you go along with it. If the matter is so important to you that you're considering divorce, tell this to Neil as often as it takes to make sure he gets it. He should not experience your leaving him, if it comes to that, as "out of the blue."

Since you're married today, view your relationship with Neil as a laboratory in which you experiment with new ways to make yourself heard and observe what happens. Look upon your problems with Neil as an opportunity to get to know your needs and desires better, and to develop new ways of communicating them. The bolder and more courageous you are, the more you will learn about Neil and yourself.

My Impossible Mother-in-Law

Dear Harriet:

My mother-in-law, Ethel, visits our home several times a year. In fact, she's due for a visit shortly. I'm not going to sugarcoat it; she's an obnoxious and critical woman and she drives me crazy. She blames me, not her son, Alec, for every imperfection she can find in our home and in our children. I've told Alec many times to tell her to shape up or stay away. But he just defends her and does nothing. We fight about her constantly and it's tearing our marriage apart. Is there anything I can do?

Dear Reader:

You are describing an all-too-common in-law triangle. When people marry, it's not uncommon for there to be negative intensity between the wife and her mother-in-law. Typically, the two women spar with each other while the man stays outside the ring.

This effectively obscures the real problem, which is not in your relationship with your mother-in-law but in your husband's relationship with his mother. Whenever one finds a wife and mother-in-law slugging it out, one finds a husband and mother who aren't addressing the emotional issues between them. Alec may be angry at his mother, too, but he won't recognize or deal with his anger because he's too busy defending her in response to your criticism. If you continue to criticize either of them, you will only succeed in reinforcing your outside position and maintaining the status quo.

Your first challenge is to lighten up, because emotional intensity only breeds more emotional intensity. Can you go three months without criticizing Alec's mother? Three weeks? Three minutes? Right now, you're protecting Alec by doing the "feeling work" for the two of you. If *all* you can do is criticize Ethel, *all* Alec may do is defend her. Observe what happens when you stop criticizing Ethel and instead comment on her competence and good points. You might find that Alec feels freer to acknowledge her difficult qualities.

When things are calm, it will then be easier to talk to Alec about the difficult time you are having with his mother's disapproval. Share your feelings without blaming Alec or Ethel and without telling him what to do. Take responsibility for your part of the problem and invite his perspective. ("Alec, I think that I overreact to Ethel and you underreact to her. Do you think there's a connection here?")

Learn more about Alec's history of expressing his differences with his mother. Can he take a clear position with Ethel about things that matter? Does he think he can say no to her? Try to recognize and support the importance of Alec's relationship with his mother. He will feel paralyzed if he hears you asking him to choose between his mother and you. Alec's challenge is to begin to connect with his mother in ways that are mutually enhancing and that do not operate at anyone's expense.

If Alec becomes motivated to change *his* part in the triangle, he can begin by establishing more of an emotional connection with his mother. For example, he can make sure to have some time alone with her during each visit. If his mother feels she's getting her due, she'll be less threatened by your relationship. And Alec will have the opportunity to practice asserting himself around the "easy" issues before tackling a big one.

Then, when Alec feels truly ready, he can tell Ethel directly that he loves both of you and that it is painful for him to hear her run you down when she visits. He can do this in the spirit of sharing his feelings, rather than delivering ultimatums.

He could also try teasing Ethel about whether she sees him as a weakling ("Mom, I wonder if you think my wife is the only strong one in the family. How come you're able to criticize *her* and not *me*?"). The triangle is more likely to loosen up if Alec can approach Ethel with humor rather than blame ("Well, to tell you the truth, Mom, it *does* make my life easier when I can lie low and watch the two of you slug it out. But I also want you and me to have a relationship where we can talk about our differences as frankly as possible").

> Whenever one finds a wife and mother-in-law slugging it out, one finds a husband and mother who aren't addressing their own relationship issues.

Most important of all, ease up on Ethel. When she visits next, try to deflect her criticisms with humor. If you're feeling especially courageous, you can move toward her by soliciting and acknowledging her perspective on homemaking and child rearing. Once you're feeling calmer and less apt to blame her, you can tell Ethel directly that it's hard for you to feel criticized by her because you respect her opinion and she's important to you and to the children.

Substantive change in families is a slow process, but the good news is that even a small change will make a big difference in your life.

Can a Vibrator Harm My Sex Life?

≋

Dear Harriet:

I'm afraid that if I start using a vibrator to masturbate, I'll stop enjoying sex with my husband. Is this a risk? Also, can the frequent use of a vibrator dry up my sex drive?

Dear Reader:

No form of masturbation will impede your ability to enjoy sex with your husband—any more than listening to music on the radio will turn you off to a live concert. As for "drying up" your sex drive, the opposite is generally true. The more sex we engage in, the more we tend to want it. The less sex we engage in, the less we tend to want it. In fact, masturbation is often encouraged by sex therapists for people who are feeling sexually inhibited or disinterested, as a way of improving their enjoyment of sex with their partners.

> No, a vibrator won't dry up your sex drive.

My Doctor Says I'm Depressed

Dear Harriet:

I'm stuck in an unhappy marriage. I can't imagine ever loving and respecting my husband or feeling good about myself when I'm with him. What's most painful is that I'm unable to make a firm decision about staying or leaving. I've been seeing a psychiatrist twice weekly for two years, but it's not helping. Now he wants to put me on medication for depression, even though I think I'm functioning well enough without it. I'm mostly concerned that pills will dull my real feelings and keep me treading water in a marriage that I really should leave. Is that possible?

Dear Reader:

Your reservations about medication deserve your attention and respect. Depression, like anger, is a signal worth listening to, as it can indicate the necessity for self-exploration and change. Depression can reflect the body's search for truth, forcing a more honest appraisal of the self, including the degree to which one is living in accord with one's authentic values and desires.

As writer Kat Duff puts it, "Sometimes I think we would lose ourselves altogether if it were not for our stubborn, irrepressible symptoms, calling us, requiring us, to re-collect ourselves and reorient ourselves to life." Women, in particular, must rely on this source of wisdom, because we are socialized to pretend, to settle, to deny that unfair circumstances exist or matter, and to call our compromises "life." Our bodies are harder to fool.

However, I don't think depression is useful if we're

drowning in it. Nor do I see virtue in suffering. Symptoms are not just wake-up calls. They can also disable us. When this happens, medication can take the edge off depression, allowing us to work more effectively in psychotherapy rather than disconnecting us from what is real. Sometimes medication helps people gain the clarity and strength we need to make necessary and difficult life changes. "It takes the rocks out of your backpack," says a psychiatrist (and hiker) friend of mine who prescribes antidepressants with good results.

> I don't think depression is useful if we're drowning in it. Nor do I see virtue in suffering.

Some experts view female depression as a normal response to injustice, inequality, and trauma. As such, it is not only a private dilemma but also a collective one, as political as it is personal. Other experts view depression as a disease for which medication is the only cure. We do know that depression is often the body's response to imbalance—be it an imbalance of blood sugar, sleep patterns, neurotransmitters, or the distribution of power in relationships.

We don't have a clue about how the widespread and continued use of mood-altering drugs will affect a given individual over the course of the life cycle, to say nothing of the implications for the evolution of the human species over the long haul. We do know, though, that antidepressant medication helps some people quite a bit, especially when it's combined with a large dose of insight, clarity, and the courage to act on one's own behalf. When depression is debilitating, antidepressants are a clearly indicated tool that can make the difference between life and death.

Medication aside, consider a few questions about your

marital situation. Have you invited your husband to join you in marital therapy? Have you been as clear as possible with him that you're thinking about divorce? Have you told him what needs to change in order for you to feel good about him and your relationship? Have you considered one or two things you can do to improve your marriage?

Finally, if therapy isn't helping you, why do you stay? Depending on how we use it, long-term psychotherapy, like medication, can enhance—or impede—our capacity to take clear action on our own behalf. Women can get stuck in therapy, just as in marriage.

In order to make a wise choice for yourself, continue the conversation about medication with your psychiatrist and gather whatever information you can from different sources. Talk straight to both your psychiatrist and your husband about your expectations and dissatisfactions with each of them. Then take whatever time you need to get clear about staying or moving on in both arenas.

I'm More Successful Than My Husband

Dear Harriet:

My husband, Phillip, and I are both talented, ambitious people who up until now have been supportive of rather than competitive with each other when it comes to our careers. Recently, however, I've experienced some remarkable successes and was even honored at a large banquet. My husband's career, in contrast, is at a standstill, and since the banquet he's been moody and distant. I've told him he's jealous, but he denies it. What can I do about his sulking? I fear that if I continue to succeed, I will lose him. I have to admit I do have competitive feelings with Phillip, and I wonder if these feelings, as well as his reaction to my success, are normal.

Dear Reader:

Feeling competitive (especially with those we are close to) is normal and universal. It's also understandable that a woman may feel anxious about her competitive spirit because it violates the rules of the game that we grew up with.

Women are encouraged to cultivate competitive feelings *for* men but to deny our competitive feelings *with* men. In fact, most of us have been taught to bolster and protect men's self-esteem at our own expense. A woman, we are taught, must be smart enough to catch a man but must never seem to outsmart him.

As a result, many women unconsciously fear that their success will threaten rather than enhance their intimate relationships, especially with men. Such fears are not unfounded or irrational. Although most intelligent and ambitious men value these same qualities in their mates, they tend to marry women who have a lower professional status and who make less money.

If this traditional arrangement shifts mid-course, the change may generate enormous stress. We all learn what the culture teaches us, which is that the man is the primary breadwinner and it's his career that really counts. It's common for men to feel diminished if the balance of economic and social power begins to shift in marriage, because the old gender rules die hard. Moreover, a career move forward or upward by one spouse (or even a close friend or colleague) inevitably puts the other in touch with his or her own feelings of "stuckness" at work.

So what can you do about it? Give Phillip some space. Don't try to change or "fix" his sulkiness. Phillip has a right to his feelings, and over time he will probably manage them just fine. Keep in mind that no one has ever died of sulking, and few people sulk forever.

Of course, giving Phillip emotional space doesn't mean lapsing into a cool or angry distance yourself. It just means that you stay connected to him without trying to rescue him from his feelings. Since Phillip denies that he is feeling jealous, it won't help to make further interpretations, but you can still keep the lines of communication open by speaking about your thoughts and feelings—not his.

You might say, for example, "Phillip, ever since the banquet, I've been experiencing you as more distant. I'm afraid that my recent successes are the cause, and I'm worried that if I get too successful, I might lose you. I think about my mother and sister, who had no career plans of their own and who always put their man's career first, and I realize that I have no models for what we're trying to achieve together." If you keep the conversation going, you might learn that Phillip is also afraid of losing you, especially if your success continues and he doesn't move forward in his own work.

Remember that Phillip chose a bright, ambitious woman as his spouse, so he obviously values the very qualities that now seem to threaten him. Try to have faith in his ability to manage his reactions over time. Phillip's initial reaction to your success doesn't mean that he won't handle things well over the long haul.

Even in the best of marriages, the situation you describe will generate anxiety, so try to deal with your situation more flexibly and with humor. Each of you will do better if you stay focused on your personal work goals and life plan rather than becoming overfocused on each other. You and Phillip are pioneers who are working along with the rest of us to create new definitions of what it means to be a man and woman in the arenas of both love and work. It is exciting and enriching—but always stressful—to forge new ground.

> A move upward by one spouse inevitably puts the other in touch with his or her own feelings of "stuckness" at work.

What Should We Name the Baby?

≈≈

Dear Harriet:

My husband and I are committed to equality in our marriage. I'm pregnant now with our first child, and I want to give the baby a hyphenated surname. Both sets of in-laws are protesting, though, saying we are complicating the child's life, since he or she may one day marry someone who also has a hyphenated name. If this happened, the next hyphenated generation would have four surnames. I don't want to compromise my values, but the problem does seem insolvable.

Dear Reader:

Choosing a baby's surname is the point at which even the most uncompromising feminist will compromise. Many folks are completely committed to equality until the baby comes—and then it's the man's name that counts.

Even women who are adamant about keeping their birth names at marriage have difficulty facing the baby-naming dilemma with an eye toward finding an egalitarian solution. If you ask a feminist why her child doesn't carry her last name, you'll typically get some variant of "for the child's sake" or "because it was so important to *him*" (or his/my family, and so on) or "my last name is just my father's name anyway." There are countless excuses, but these are the top three I usually hear.

My point is not that feminist mothers should all be radical pioneers and ensure that our children carry our birth name (although why not?). This is a personal decision each woman must make for herself. But we do need to scrutinize our own feelings on the subject rather than bringing in the apparent needs of children, in-laws, husbands, parents, or the world in general.

Why are we unwilling to oppose sexist solutions? Imagine a cultural tradition in business that went like this: whenever a black person and a white person hold a business in common, the business will be given the white person's name. There is no justification for this—expedience, necessity, history, or tradition—that wouldn't be recognized as racist and deemed unacceptable. Institutionalized racism matters. So, too, does institutionalized sexism.

So what to do? We can avoid the subject entirely by holding on to old excuses ("Rodriguez-Margulis won't fit on a computer card—and what will happen when she marries Rosenbaum-Lazarino?"). We can adopt a compromise solution such as using our birth name as a child's middle name, which is a step forward but still protects the status quo. Or we can acknowledge that patriarchal values still run deep in our feminist bones—and redouble our efforts to find creative solutions to the baby-naming problem.

Just in case I have managed to instill guilt in those of you who didn't dare or don't want to, I should mention that Lerner is my husband's name. Happily, there are good examples all around me: When my colleagues Jeanine Roembach and Greg Clark married, they each changed their surname to Roembach-Clark to keep their family name unified. If and when their children marry, perhaps their daughters will keep the name Roembach and their son the name Clark.

> Choosing a baby's surname is the point at which even the most uncompromising feminists compromise.

My friends Judie Koontz and Chuck Baird don't like hyphens. They named their daughter Zoey Baird Koontz. A son would have had Chuck's surname and been Koontz Baird.

When my friends Tom Averill and Jeffrey Ann Goudie had a daughter, they named her Eleanor Goudie-Averill and became, as Jeffrey puts it, "one family with three separate-but-equal last names." Eleanor takes pride in having both of her parents names, although it initially took her a while to understand that one of her names was not Hyphen.

So what should you do? I have no pat answers. I'm not even a good example. But since working with families is my stock-in-trade, I can say one thing for certain: children handle their business just fine (hyphens included) when we are able to take care of our own.

I'm Not a Failure

≋

Dear Harriet:

My husband and I grew apart after seventeen years of marriage and embarked on an amicable divorce. I regret neither our marriage nor its end. What angers me are people who refer to my "failed marriage." How can I convince them that ending my marriage doesn't make me, or my husband, or our many good years together, a failure.

Dear Reader:

Your words remind me of the late anthropologist Margaret Mead who was asked to account for her three "failed marriages." She responded that she didn't have three failed marriages but rather three successful marriages for three different developmental stages of her life.

Negative stereotypes about divorce linger on, even though our 50 percent divorce rate makes divorce a normative life-cycle stage in our society. When a couple divorces, it sends shock waves through other people's marriages. Those who pejoratively refer to your failed marriage may not wish to confront their own marital problems or the fact that no marriage is divorce-proof.

Many people are quicker to find failure in those who divorce without regret than in those who remain stuck in an unhappy situation. It's unlikely that you can convince other people to change or even to examine their views on the subject. Instead, the challenge for each of us is to live as well as we can by our values, without getting too caught up in what other people think.

Choosing to Be Childless

Dear Harriet:

I am constantly defending myself and offering explanations to people who think that something is wrong with me because my husband and I have chosen to be childless. Am I really missing out, or do you think that a childless woman can live a totally fulfilled life? And how can I convince my critics?

Dear Reader:

Stop trying to convince your critics. The more you try to offer lengthy arguments on your own behalf, the more defensive you will sound. Just let people know—lightly or humorously, if possible—that it's your choice. Let their reaction be their own problem.

All women have been raised with the message that we should *want* to have children. But women do differ from one another. To assume that women should all be mothers is like assuming that all men should be accountants because they're supposedly better at math. Even the term *childless* (as compared to *child-free*) reflects our lingering negative attitudes toward women who do not reproduce.

Forty (40) percent of American women between the ages of eighteen and forty-four do not have children. Are you missing out by being among them? Of course. But women who *do* have children also miss out. Every significant life choice is a mixed bag that precludes other experiences and choices.

Should I Stay or Should I Go?

Dear Harriet:

I feel as if I've been in therapy forever, trying to decide whether or not to leave my husband. As soon as I'm certain I want a divorce I begin to panic about how I'd survive economically, how lonely I'd be, or how furious my children would be at me. When I decide to stay I become depressed because I don't want to spend the rest of my life with my husband. My therapist encourages me to work on the marriage, and my friends think I should get out. Of course, you don't know my situation, but could you comment on my inability to make a final decision and stick to it? That's what's really torturing me.

Dear Reader:

Many people, like yourself, struggle for a very long time before they gather the courage to separate or divorce—or before they gather the courage to stay, for that matter. Since you're not ready to make a final decision, it doesn't help to get caught up in self-criticism. Nor will other people, including your therapist, have the answer for you. It's important to take all the time you need to get clear about your situation and to test out how much potential your marriage has for positive change.

Since you're married today, focus on strengthening yourself both in and out of this relationship. Here are several ideas to consider.

1. Work toward having a life plan that does not require marriage for your emotional and financial

survival. For example, if you were divorced or widowed tomorrow, what new skills or areas of expertise would you need to acquire? Begin to acquire them now. You might decide to return to school to improve your economic prospects. You might increase your confidence in driving alone to new places. You might begin managing 50 percent of the marital assets that would be legally yours if you did divorce.

2. Create a rich and enduring network of relationships. You will obviously need the support of friends, family, and community if your marriage ends, but you also need the support of these relationships to make your marriage work. If you're isolated or cut off, your marriage will be all the more intense and overloaded. Strengthen your connections to the important people in your life.

3. Work to bring more of your authentic self to your marriage. This means talking openly with your husband about important emotional issues (including your struggle about staying or leaving); defining your values, beliefs, convictions, and principles, and keeping your behavior consistent with them; taking a clear position on where you stand on important issues; clarifying what is acceptable and tolerable to you in the relationship; defining the limits of what you can comfortably do or give.

4. Clarify your bottom line. What are your deepest values and beliefs about what you expect from—or deserve in—marriage? How far can you depart from

> The more prepared you are to live
> without your husband, if need be—
> the more freely you can choose to stay.

these? At what point do you say, "Enough!" and refuse
to continue with business as usual until a change
occurs? There is no "right" bottom line for all women.
But if you have *no* bottom line ("There's just no way I
can leave him until the children are grown"), your
marriage and your self-respect will be severely compromised. The more prepared you are to live without
your husband, if need be—the more freely you can
choose to stay.

Every bold and courageous step you take on your own
behalf will allow you to know yourself, your husband, and
your relationship better. That's a worthwhile venture—
whether or not you stay together over the long haul.

7

≋

Parents in Recovery

Introduction

Before I had children, I was amazed at the improper behavior of the mothers I observed. I knew when I gazed into the eyes of my own newborn son that I would never yell at him in the supermarket line, or tell him to go watch television, or feed him McDonald's hamburgers. I certainly wouldn't be a worrier like my mother. I wouldn't picture him kidnapped or dead in a ditch just because he disappeared for a while or I couldn't track him down.

Of course I did all these things and more that I never imagined. Nothing is more humbling than becoming a parent, because until we have children we don't have a clue about what they will evoke in us. Motherhood caught me entirely unprepared for the range and intensity of feelings I would experience toward my two sons. I didn't know I was capable of feeling such exhaustion, protectiveness, or love, or such intense bursts of rage. Nor did I know how frightened I would feel at the thought that something bad would happen to them, how quickly I would imagine disaster.

Motherhood has become easier for me with age—
both mine and my kids'. Some mothers hate to see their
babies grow up, but I am not among them. My sons, Matt
and Ben, are in college and high school, respectively. I love
the fact that they dress themselves, use the toilet, and make
interesting conversation. I'm pleased that they are largely
responsible for their own safety and that some act of care-
lessness on my part, like leaving a sharp object within their
reach, will not endanger them. Sometimes I miss their
babyhood, the pure, fierce physicality of that earlier relationship. But I'm glad those years are behind me.

When Matt was only several weeks old, a neighborhood woman, probably in her sixties, stopped by to solicit
funds for a local charity. I was exhausted, having been up
most of the night unable to comfort him. As she bent over
his sleeping body, she commented on how sweet he
smelled. "Yes," I said, "God gives all babies their own special smell so that their mothers won't throw them out the
window in the middle of the night." I thought I was being
funny, but from my neighbor's tense silence and quick
exit, I realized that I had made an error of social judgment. I had, although in jest, alluded to feelings of violence in motherhood.

My friends and I take for granted our frank conversations about mothering. But my own mother, like my
shocked neighbor, had no such opportunity. Their generation of women felt like monsters when they raged at their
children or expressed dissatisfaction with their "sacred calling." Back then, the "good mother" played by the rules
and selflessly dedicated herself to her children. She had
only herself to blame for her unhappiness.

Guilt and self-blame have long been occupational hazards of motherhood. When my boys were young, women
were still on the receiving end of contradictory, dispiriting
messages from experts who were themselves neither
women nor mothers. "Working mothers" were warned that

their children, deprived of constant maternal attention, would not grow. "Housewives" were accused of dominating and controlling their children to compensate for their own unhappy lives. Although motherhood was shrouded in an aura of sentimentality, homemakers were depicted in the media as idiots who drooled over their newly waxed floors and were said not to work. Mothers were held responsible for everything that went wrong in family life.

But to these guilt-inducing pronouncements, mothers now say "Enough!" I hear less these days from women who worry about the psychological effects of their employment on children, although they may be sorry to leave them. Instead, both parents may be worrying about finding a job with good health insurance, or about losing the job they have. Or mothers opt for the traditional stay-at-home path but may pay a price down the road. It's just common sense that when children come along *both* parents need to scale down their ambitions and work less, to make room for family life, but the resistance to changing the old roles runs deep.

We attend best to the needs of children when we view their problems through the widest possible lens. Today we hear more about "parenting skills" and "family systems," a definite improvement over the earlier narrow focus on perfecting and improving mothers. There's a growing focus on societal inequities and work pressures that shape family relationships and affect children profoundly. Although the notion of "women and children first" has always enjoyed a kind of bumper sticker popularity, mothers and children remain to this day the most economically unprotected group in the United States.

Parents tell me today how much they want their sons and daughters to survive, to find a place in the world, and maybe to grab a little dignity along the way—and how afraid they are that this won't happen. To make it happen, we need to look realistically and respectfully at the many circumstances in which children grow up. In our country, single mothers, divorced mothers, poor mothers, remarried mothers, lesbian mothers, stepmothers, mothers of color, and disabled mothers taken altogether are the vast majority and therefore the face of American mothers.

Every category of mothers needs respect, economic protection, recognition, institutional support, and connection to family and friends who care about them. Fathers, too. This, along with occasional good advice, is what helps kids most.

Do I Have to Breast-Feed My Baby?

Dear Harriet:

Help! I'm writing this letter from the hospital where I just had my first baby, Rosalie. I don't want to breast-feed her, but my pediatrician says that it's essential to her mental and physical health. He says bottle-fed babies do poorly and that all mothers enjoy nursing. Every cell in my body rebels against the idea of breast-feeding, but I'm dying of guilt. Is breast-feeding necessary? Do all "normal" mothers want to nurse their babies?

Dear Reader:

There is nothing that *all* mothers want to do, in regard to nursing or any other aspect of parenting. Women are different from one another. Your baby will not suffer from being bottle-fed. Rather, she might benefit from having a mother who respects herself and considers her own feelings.

The literature on infancy does suggest that there are benefits to breast-feeding babies, because mother's milk contains antibodies that help protect infants during their first six months, when they have little immunologic defense. Research studies comparing breast-fed and bottle-fed youngsters have shown that those who were breast-fed have relatively fewer instances of respiratory infections, diarrhea, eczema, asthma, hay fever, and miscellaneous infections. In addition, breast-feeding provides some mothers with a uniquely gratifying opportunity for emotional and physical closeness to their baby.

That said, babies who are bottle-fed lovingly and affectionately grow up just fine. Infants need lots of cuddling and touch, but breast-feeding is not the only way to provide intimate contact. The guilt and insecurity instilled in mothers by experts (most of whom are neither women nor mothers) are far more detrimental to babies than the actual limitations of infant formula.

To gain a broader perspective on your own feelings, consider learning more about the history of breast-feeding and infant care in your own family. Did your mother breast-feed, and what was her experience? How did she decide between the breast and the bottle? Do you know what might account for your own aversion to breast-feeding? When we know our family history on a particular issue, we can make more informed choices in our own life.

Talk to friends as well so that you can begin to appreciate the diversity of women's experience as mothers. And if your pediatrician doesn't respect and support your choices, consider finding a new one. It is your doctor's job to give you all the facts to consider and to make a recommendation. But it is not your doctor's job to judge your mothering. You should be commended for listening to your own strong inner voice at a time when women are most vulnerable to submitting to authority at their own expense.

Rest assured that whatever hardships Rosalie faces later in life will not be caused by a lack of breast milk. I wish that all the experts who try to create perfect mothers would turn their primary attention toward creating a humane and caring world in which families might flourish.

Try not to "die of guilt." True enough, we live in a culture that encourages women to cultivate guilt like a little flower garden. But ultimately your own self-regard and strength of character are two of the best gifts you can give your daughter.

Adoption and Self-Esteem

Dear Harriet:

After a long struggle with fertility problems, my husband, Eugene, and I adopted a baby daughter, Annie. She is so precious to us that we now feel my inability to conceive was a blessing from God. We told Annie that she was adopted when she was five. Now, at thirteen, she has low self-esteem, which her teacher suspects is related to her being adopted. Should we not have told Annie she was adopted? How can we make her understand that she is a chosen child and that our family is no different from any other?

Dear Reader:

You were right to tell Annie about her adoption. Children deserve to know the facts about their birth and about how they entered their family. When secrecy surrounds adoption it leads to distance and disorientation in the family, and to relationships built on deception rather than trust.

As with any emotionally charged subject, adoption can and should be discussed calmly and frankly at all stages of family life. As children mature, they raise new questions about their adoption; or the same question changes in meaning over time. For example, "Who is my mother?" means one thing to a kindergarten child and another to an adolescent girl trying to clarify her identity and make sense of her world.

Reconsider your wish to convince Annie that her family is "no different from any other." Such a perspective is neither useful nor true. It's entirely understandable that your loving concern for her would be expressed this way because the process of adoption has been based on a denial of differences. Adoption policies have been guided by the principle that biological and adoptive families are exactly the same. This creates denial and the suppression of facts and feelings for all involved—the adoptee, the adoptive parents, and the birth parents.

It is normal for Annie to experience a range of feelings about her adoption. She may feel joy, gratitude, loyalty, and satisfaction, as well as loss, grief, shame, anger, and confusion. It is also normal for Annie to grieve over her loss of significant people, her separation from the mother who gave her life, and the possibility that she may never meet her birth parents. If she decides to search for them when she is older, she may also react emotionally if she isn't given access to important facts. Despite growing pressure for adoption reform, the laws of our land still seal adoption records in all but a handful of states.

> Children deserve to know the facts
> about their birth and about how
> they entered their family.

Just as Annie needs to come to terms with her varied emotions, I would encourage you and Eugene to deal as openly as possible with your own feelings about infertility and adoption. If the two of you have not yet grieved together over the loss of the biological child you once fantasized having, it will be difficult for you to acknowledge the entire range of Annie's feelings. If you feel guilty for "causing" Annie's low self-esteem by having adopted her, you might be overcompensating by overfocusing on her specialness. Annie knows that adoption was not your first choice, so your insistence that she is your "chosen child" might seem confusing or less than honest to her.

The most important challenge for you and Eugene is to create a calm emotional climate where Annie feels safe to ask questions and share her feelings. All families, no matter how they came together, face a similar challenge.

Moreover, try to remember that children feel angry, rejected, confused, and sad in countless emotional circumstances other than adoption. Adolescent girls routinely struggle mightily to maintain their self-regard and their sense of authentic identity, so don't assume a single source for Annie's low self-esteem. Overfocusing on the adoption issue is as troublesome as ignoring it altogether.

Does My Son Need
a Man in the House?

Dear Harriet:

My loving husband died two years ago, and I'm raising our seven-year-old son, Josh, by myself. We are both doing well, but I'm worried that Josh will become a "Mama's boy" with no man in the house. I read somewhere that a mother interferes with her son's masculine development if she's overly close to him. Should I keep my distance from Josh, so he won't identify with my feminine qualities? Can I love my son too much?

Dear Reader:

Sure, any parent can be invasive, domineering, intrusive, and controlling to a son or daughter's detriment. But you cannot love your son too much.

Twenty-five (25) percent of children under the age of eighteen live in single-parent households. Boys are usually with their mothers, and do not suffer from this arrangement.

Instead, boys suffer from the false notion that they should grow up to be as *unlike* their mothers as possible. And mothers suffer from the myth that they can "feminize" or "contaminate" their sons by too much closeness. On the practical side, female-headed households often suffer from poverty, which isn't good for anybody's relationship or mental health.

What terrible "feminine qualities" do you think your son might absorb from you? Your commitment to being a good parent? The strength you demonstrate by your ability to love and care for your son in the aftermath of great loss? Your tenderness and sensitivity? Consider the possibility that Josh can benefit from identifying with the good qualities of his mother. In this light, I heartily endorse the work of family therapist Olga Silverstein whose book, *The Courage to Raise Good Men*, dispels the myth that only a father can make a boy a man or that over-closeness between mothers and sons is a bad thing.

> Any parent can be invasive, domineering, intrusive, and controlling, but you cannot love your son too much.

That said, the untimely loss of a parent is one of the most difficult emotional challenges for a family to come to terms with, and no parent and child should be isolated in a tight emotional circle of grief. We all need multiple connections with other family members, including aunts, uncles, cousins, and grandparents. Kids do best when they are richly connected to their roots, and you can keep the memory of Josh's father alive for him through stories, rituals, and regular contact with your deceased husband's family.

You and Josh have suffered an immeasurable loss. The best thing you can do right now is to follow your heart and give your son all the love and closeness that he most certainly needs.

Helping a Child with Divorce

≈≈

Dear Harriet:

I recently ended my marriage because my husband was unable to express his feelings or talk about his problems. Now I'm worried that my ten-year-old son, Jay, is becoming exactly like his father. I'm doing everything I can to get him to talk about the fear and anger he may be experiencing, but he clams up—just the way his father did for fifteen years. Should I put Jay in therapy?

Dear Reader:

Dealing with divorce—or any major emotional event—is a difficult, long-term process. Try to have faith in Jay's ability to cope with the changes in his family as well as to manage his feelings and make his own choices about what he wants to talk about—and with whom. Respect his need for privacy and his own sense of timing.

There is no one right way to manage stress. Children handle it in a variety of ways. Some are quick to share their feelings and seek close emotional contact, while others seek privacy and distance. Each of these coping styles is normal, yet both can trouble parents.

You obviously want a relationship with your son that involves openly expressing thoughts and feelings. But Jay may need some emotional space, and he will only distance himself more if you continue to urge him to open up. Perhaps the best help you can give Jay is to lighten up some without distancing yourself from him. First and foremost, Jay needs to know that you are there for him, that you support his ongoing relationship with his dad, and that he will not lose either of you.

If you blame your divorce on your ex-husband's fail-ure to acknowledge and express his feelings, it is under-standable that you don't want your son to be like his dad. But you won't gain anything by sending Jay this spoken (or unspoken) message. If Jay feels that he must deny those parts of himself that remind you of his father, he will have an even harder time moving toward you.

> We can't demand that our children share
> their feelings with us. We can only help
> create an emotional climate that
> fosters self-disclosure.

Paradoxically, Jay may need your permission to be *like* his dad (that is, to be private rather than self-disclosing) so that he can eventually feel comfortable deciding to be *dif-ferent* from him. If Jay feels that resembling—or respect-ing—his dad is a betrayal or disappointment to you, he will find it especially difficult to navigate the divorce process and open up to you over time.

You might want to consider therapy for yourself rather than for Jay. You are far more capable of making changes that will significantly alter the emotional climate of your family's relationships than is your ten-year-old son. Therapy can help you broaden your perspective on what went wrong in your marriage—as well as what went right—and to clarify your own part in that process.

The more you focus your primary energy on your own issues, the less likely you will be to maintain a worried or overcritical focus on Jay or his dad. In the meantime, keep in mind that we can't demand that our children share their feelings with us. We can only help create an emotional atmosphere that fosters honest self-disclosure.

Should We Allow Our Teenager to Bring Pornography Home?

Dear Harriet:

Our thirteen-year-old son has been bringing the sleaziest porno magazine into our house. I'm a feminist and this upsets me to no end. My husband says I can't forbid him to buy it, because that would only make him want to read it more. I would very much like to know how you would personally handle this behavior if it occurred in your own family, because it's driving me crazy.

Dear Reader:

I would tell my son that I wasn't comfortable having the magazines in the house and that it was against the family rules. I'd briefly share with him why it troubled me, how the magazines made me feel, and why I didn't want them in my home.

At the same time, I would let him know that I considered it his responsibility, not mine, to decide what to read. Even if I wanted to control his literary choices, I wouldn't have the power to do so. My message would be that I have some rules about what is brought into our home—but it's his job to clarify his values on this matter, which may be different from mine. I'd also keep in mind that a lot of thirteen-year-old boys go through a porn phase that has more to do with their friends than with their actual sexual attitudes toward women.

I would try to deal with the situation as calmly as possible, so that my son's interest in the magazine would not

> ## We don't have the power to control the literary choices of our children.

be enhanced by my negative focus on his choice of reading material. If he continued to buy it but stashed it at a friend's house, that would be his choice. Regardless, I would hope that we could talk together about our respective values and beliefs on the subject. And I'd trust that in time, he'd upgrade his literary tastes.

Should We Let Our Son Sleep in Our Bed?

Dear Harriet:

Is it unhealthy for little kids to sleep in their parents' bed? We try to get our eight-year-old to sleep in his own room, but he often wakes up in the middle of the night and says he's scared of being alone. He then cries until we bring him into our bed. Also, does it hurt a child occasionally to see his parents making love?

Dear Reader:

Families tend to function better when kids and parents have separate beds. If your son wakes up frightened, you or your husband can take turns staying with him until he falls asleep. This solution will be harder for you in the short run but easier for everyone over the long haul. You should also give your son lots of opportunity to tell you what he is afraid of and what he thinks about when he gets scared. Talk with your husband about when the problem began and what events or changes in the family may have triggered your son's anxiety.

Once you've decided that your son can no longer join you in bed, tell him the new rule and stick with it ("I will sit with you at night if you're feeling scared or upset. But from now on, you'll be sleeping in your own bed. Our bed is just for me and your dad to sleep in"). Remember, too, that if you give in after a long period of your son's crying, you will be teaching him that sustained crying will eventually get him what he wants, which is not a precedent any parent wants to set.

> As for making love when your son is in your bed—don't do it.

Keep in mind that it is normal and necessary for a child to test a new rule any number of times to see whether parents are really serious about it. Set limits with warmth and without criticizing or blaming your son for his feelings or reactions. He has the right to be upset about the new rule, and you have the right to stand behind it.

As for making love when your son is in your bed: don't do it, even if you're convinced he's asleep. You cannot be certain that he is really asleep, or that he won't wake up, or even that he will be totally unaware of it if he is asleep. Sexual activity between parents is too intense, stimulating, and anxiety-provoking for a child to observe.

Clarifying rules and boundaries is a challenge for all parents. It's harder still if our own parents had difficulty with this same task—if we grew up in a family characterized by rigid authoritarian rules or in a family that operated like a glob of protoplasm, without clear parental leadership and generational boundaries. Kids do best when parents are calm, clear, and consistent about family rules, so all parents should try to stand firmly behind their decisions, while keeping open minds in the light of new facts and information.

Talking to Children About
Illness and Death

Dear Harriet:

My two daughters, ages eight and thirteen, are very close to my mother, who is terminally ill. Should I tell the girls that she is dying, and include them in her funeral? My bossy older sister gave a definite no to both questions, but I think my thirteen-year-old can handle it. What do you think?

Dear Reader:

Dealing with death and loss is the most difficult task that families confront. It is also the most inevitable and inescapable of all life's challenges. Eventually, we must all confront the loss of family members as well as our own death. It has been said that we are dying from the moment we are born, or, put another way, that life itself is a sexually transmitted terminal condition.

Parents often deal with their own anxiety about loss by "protecting" their children through secrecy or silence. Although this may lower anxiety in the present, it shuts down the lines of communication and creates more serious problems over the long haul. Children have a need to grieve, too, and we don't have to rush in to fix it for them or smooth things over.

Children react best when their parents are clear and factual about death and when all members of the family are allowed to take part in good-byes and death rituals. You can encourage both your children to visit their grandmother before she dies and to attend her funeral as well. Children, like adults, deal better with reality than with their unchecked fantasies about death, which will surely flourish if they are excluded from the grief process.

You can also help your children to work through this important loss by openly sharing your own sadness about your mother's dying. Obviously, you shouldn't use the children as your therapist or overload them with your emotional intensity. But if you underreact to this important loss by concealing real feelings, your children are likely to overreact to it.

> Children react best when their parents are clear and factual about death.

Meanwhile, try to respect your sister's different coping style. Don't tell her what to do, and don't justify your own actions. Just let her know that because individuals are different, you and she might handle the same painful situation in a different way.

Losing a parent is a particularly stressful time in the family's life cycle. Because anxiety runs so high, the ground is fertile for you and your sister to get stuck in nonproductive positions of distancing or blaming. Sisters and brothers frequently get angry at each other after the death of a parent, perhaps as an unconscious attempt to detour the intense feelings surrounding the loss.

You and your sister need each other for mutual support, so do your part to maintain the best possible relationship with her. If she usually manages her own anxiety by taking charge, simply expect that she will be bossier than ever during this difficult time.

Breaking a Promise

Dear Harriet:

After my divorce, I promised my teenage daughters that I would never date someone they disliked. Now I'm dating a man they think is obnoxious, and they're trying to hold me to my promise. I've taught my daughters not to lie or break promises. But I really like this guy. I'm incredibly torn apart.

Dear Reader:

Apologize to your daughters for making a promise that you can't keep. If they're angry at you for "lying," then validate their right to be angry, but don't dwell on the problem.

Your kids have every right to be angry with you for breaking your promise. But you also have the right to change your mind. They have the right to dislike this guy (although not to be rude to him); you have the right to date him. Listen to your children and empathize with their feelings without trying to change their minds or make them see things your way.

Promises should not be made—or broken—lightly. But they are not carved in stone. Your earlier promise to your children may have been inspired by your feelings of anxiety and guilt about your divorce, rather than by carefully thinking about your own values and life plan. Say you're sorry and move on.

Our Son Says He's Gay

Dear Harriet:

Our nineteen-year-old son, Ralph, recently told my husband and me that he is homosexual. Apparently, his sexual fantasies and attractions have always involved males only. He says his attempts to have sex with women have been depressing failures. We are devastated that he won't marry. Should we send him to a psychiatrist to help him interact successfully with women before it's too late?

Dear Reader:

Parents of gay children often experience shock, sorrow, and disbelief before they are able to feel genuine acceptance. It is understandably painful for you to realize that your son will never have a conventional life, and that your picture of his future must be revised.

Ralph's sexual orientation will not change, but if he feels ashamed, guilty, or anxious enough, he may try to deny or conceal his passions, pretend to be heterosexual, even marry. If he goes this route, he will also become depressed, as happens when we live false and joyless lives. And in the process he may devastate the woman he tries to be heterosexual with.

Does Ralph *want* to see a psychiatrist? If so, encourage him to choose one who will affirm his experience, not someone who makes false claims about "curing" homosexuality. Ralph deserves to have love and joy in his life, as well as dignity and self-regard. This may not happen if important people fail to accept his being gay or try to change him.

We all may internalize society's messages that homosexuality is shameful, sick, or bad. The fact is that homosexuality is as normal as heterosexuality, meaning there are lots of crazy and healthy folks in both groups. If part of your sadness stems from guilt, be assured that parents don't "cause" their children to become gay.

Also, don't feel alone. There are an estimated 25 million gay and lesbian people in the United States with 50 million parents and 100 million grandparents. I suggest that you and your husband contact PFLAG

> Homosexuality is as normal as heterosexuality, meaning there are lots of crazy and healthy folks in both groups.

(an acronym for Parents, Families, and Friends of Lesbians and Gays). PFLAG's national network of support groups has more than 350 local chapters and hot lines to help you during this difficult time.

Ralph doesn't need to be made to feel any more alienated than he already does. He needs his family and friends at his side. The right to be different, the right to be who we are, is the most precious right we have.

I'm Indulgent and He's Too Strict

Dear Harriet:

My husband and I cannot agree on what to feed our first and only child, Bette, who is now almost three. I think it's OK for her to eat sweets and desserts, which she totally loves. He wants her to do without sugar and to eat healthy food only. We are constantly fighting about this. What do you think is best?

Dear Reader:

What's best for Bette is to have two parents who can lighten up and reach some consensus about her care, even if they don't see eye to eye on a particular issue. You and your husband need not share the same beliefs and values about what to feed children—but you do need to establish a clear-cut policy. If you continue to fight about this, you may soon have an anxious, troubled child on your hands.

Be flexible and compromise with each other so that you can reach an agreement you can both live with.

> What's best for your daughter is to have parents who can lighten up and reach a consensus about her care.

On the one hand, Bette won't suffer from eating some sweets, but on the other, she won't suffer from going without them. She will suffer, however, if she continues to be the subject of marital intensity, or if her parents remain anxiously and excessively focused on what she does or does not eat.

Is It Ever OK to Lie to a Child

Dear Harriet:

My daughter Connie and her best friend were watching a TV show about extramarital affairs. After her friend left, Connie asked me if I had ever been "unfaithful to Dad." In truth, I did have a brief affair eight years ago. But I wanted to protect Connie, who is only thirteen, and I also worried that she would tell other people. So I lied and said no. My husband, who knows about the affair, says I shouldn't have lied to Connie, and he pointed out that we forbid her to lie to us. Was my lie justified? Must I tell my daughter the truth in every instance?

Dear Reader:

Of course you have the right to conceal some information from your daughter—and vice versa. Secrecy between the generations can reflect healthy boundaries and a need for privacy. Parents make daily decisions about what information to impart to their children and how and when to do it.

Was your lie justified? It depends on whom you ask. Even experts on families have very different beliefs about whether a particular lie is honorable, excusable, questionable, or deplorable. Work to clarify *your* opinion on the subject. Consider, too, whether lying to protect Connie is a rare and uncommon event—or whether it's habitual and reflexive.

We always have options other than lying or "telling all." Instead, you might have said lightly, "There are certain subjects that are private and my sex life is one of them." This way children learn that some aspects of their parents' lives are "nobody's business." Privacy is the most basic of human rights, protecting the dignity and ultimate separateness of each family member.

Respect the fact that Connie will keep secrets from you as well. And although you've forbidden her to lie to you, keep in mind that healthy, normal teenagers *do* occasionally lie to their parents for all the usual reasons—to avoid punishment and disapproval, to carve out a separate space, to protect a parent from worry, and to stave off unwanted intrusion, attention, and encroachment.

Do continue the conversation with your husband about your different points of view—and listen carefully to him. His readiness to let Connie know about your affair may reflect a need for the two of you to talk more about it. Perhaps he's still feeling hurt or angry. We convey information to our children (or decide not to) with the greatest clarity and calm when the issue is well processed with our adult partner.

> Privacy is the most basic of human rights, protecting the dignity and ultimate separateness of each family member.

You deserve credit for struggling with a difficult dilemma. Too many of us are on automatic pilot when it comes to lying or truth-telling. And when parents are feeling anxious, they often push the extremes, failing to tell children facts that affect them, or not protecting a child enough from adult concerns. Either extreme can cause problems.

We're All the Same on the Inside

Dear Harriet:

I'm a twenty-five-year-old white woman newly married to an African-American man, Aron, who is thirty. Our parents can't stop worrying about the fate of the children that our marriage will produce. They ask, "How will you raise them?" We answer, "As human beings," because we hope to treat them as unique individuals, not as people of a particular color or kind. In a world divided by racial hatred, don't you think this is a good idea?

Dear Reader:

In a world divided by racial hatred, it doesn't help to be color-blind. Children do best when they have clear information about their ethnic identity and take pride in their cultural heritage. Your wish to raise your children as if race doesn't matter reflects your good intentions. But in practice you can't change the fact that others will categorize your children even if you don't, and to forge their own identity your children need to feel connected to their rich cultural traditions.

Your children may feel they have to choose one identity over another if you don't take care to instill pride in and connection to their varied roots. Also, by denying the implications of their biracial identity, you won't help them deal with the racial prejudice and stereotypes they will ultimately encounter, particularly when they enter adolescence and begin to date.

If you raise your children in a predominantly white community—or if Aron is not emotionally and geographically close to his family—you'll need to make an extra effort to help your children feel connected to their African-American roots. Biracial children face the complex challenge of embracing and integrating at least two ethnic identities and distinct heritages. This is particularly difficult in a world where differences are feared, silenced— even eradicated—rather than affirmed and celebrated.

Ask yourself, how knowledgeable are you about your culture, ethnicity, and family history? *White is a color, not a culture.* Learn as much as you can about your own ethnic background and about the immigrations that brought your relatives to America. Did they come by choice or were they forced by economic or political necessity? Were ties severed or maintained with those left behind? Some whites know remarkably little about their history and culture. To help provide children with a rich and authentic sense of historical continuity, you and Aron will both benefit from gathering facts and stories from your own families.

Your parents have a point when they worry that you are beginning your marriage from a position of denial ("Color makes no difference"). Talk openly over time with

> In a world divided by racial hatred,
> it doesn't help to be color-blind.

Aron about your thoughts and feelings about marrying out of your race. Your children will be affected by your unspoken and unacknowledged feelings. You won't be able to provide clear, positive, and consistent information about both sides of their racial heritage if you avoid facing the messy complexity of your own reactions. We all internalize some messages from our racist society, and it's better to examine than to ignore them.

Finally, focusing on the fate of your children may obscure more immediate emotional issues. For example, how do Aron's parents feel about their son marrying a white woman? How do his relatives feel? What about your own family? Keep the lines of communication open about these and other emotionally loaded subjects. Remember, adults will overfocus on children (and grandchildren) when they fail to identify and address their real concerns with one another.

Introducing an Adopted Child

Dear Harriet:

We adopted our youngest child, Dan, who is now ten. In my efforts to be open about this fact, I always introduce him as "my adopted son, Dan." But this introduction bothers him. Who do you think is right?

Dear Reader:

I think you should respect Dan's feelings, even if you don't agree with him. Apart from the question of who's "right," why introduce Dan in a way that makes him feel uncomfortable?

I appreciate your wish to avoid the secrecy that so often surrounds adoption.

> Temper your desire for openness with your son's right to privacy.

But overfocusing on it isn't helpful either. Would you say, for example, "This is my biological son, Pete?"

Consider tempering your desire for openness with Dan's right to privacy, his discomfort about being set apart, and his wish to make his own decisions about how, and with whom, he will share personal information.

Telling Children Secrets

Dear Harriet:

My fourteen-year-old daughter, Cindy, can't keep a secret from her twelve-year-old sister, Meg. Most recently, I told Cindy that my mother needs open-heart surgery. This information was to remain between the two of us, but, as usual she told Meg the next day. Meg is a very sensitive child who can't deal with difficult information. I tell Cindy everything, but how can I make her keep a confidence? Punishing her hasn't helped. Please give some advice.

Dear Reader:

Cindy's problem is not that she can't keep a secret. Spilling the beans may be her way of letting you know her discomfort with *your* behavior.

Cindy is Meg's peer, not her parent. Although Cindy may derive gratification from being your confidant, it's important that she feel free to relate to her sister openly, without having to conceal information or watch herself. The secret-keeping business may place Cindy in too difficult a bind.

Naturally, you want to protect Meg from unnecessary anxiety. But the selective sharing and guarding of information across generations ("Don't tell your sister!" "Don't tell Dad!") creates "insiders" and "outsiders" in families. The negative power of secrecy derives both from the emotional importance of what is not spoken (the content) and the hidden alliances, triangles, and calls to loyalty that secrets can create (the process).

Siblings need each other. If Cindy stays in the secret-keeping business, she and Meg will become increasingly distant over time. Moreover, Cindy's own anxiety (in this case, about her grandmother's surgery) will only intensify if she is sworn to secrecy. And her position as Mother's confidant or "best friend" may set her up as an object of Meg's resentment well into adulthood.

Meg, too, is unlikely to thrive in the ongoing shadow of secrecy. Over time, she may learn not to ask, to look the other way, to blunt her curiosity, and to discount her own perceptions and intuition. Her anxiety will increase if information that is relevant to her life is mystified and concealed, if she senses your anxiety but has no way to make sense of it. Meg will also have to struggle to show her competence and strength if her family treats her as fragile by failing to include her.

Consider how you might talk to both of your daughters about their grandmother's impending surgery and other important issues that affect them. The challenge is to create a safe space where family members can ask questions and share their feelings over time.

Is secrecy always bad? Of course not. All families have some secrets that may be absolutely necessary at a particular point in family life. We keep secrets to protect, not fracture, important relationships. But the hidden costs of secrecy can be profoundly disempowering—eroding connection, blocking authentic engagement and trust, and stripping a family of spontaneity, vitality, and connection.

Children have a remarkable ability to handle difficult facts if their parents are calm and keep their own anxiety in check. Try to keep the lines of communication open and find support for yourself at this difficult time surrounding your mother's surgery. And when you want to keep information private from one of your daughters, consider telling neither.

Can Single Mothers Raise Boys?

Dear Harriet:

I am divorced and have a sixteen-year-old son, John. I'm finding it difficult to make him stick to my rules. My friends say that I should send him to stay with his father, because he needs a male role model. I don't think John would be better off with his dad, but I'm worried that the problem reflects the lack of a man in the house.

Dear Reader:

Raising a teenager is a difficult task—even more so for a single parent. Feeling inadequate is also an occupational hazard of motherhood. But the belief that single women can't raise boys only serves to undermine further a mother's confidence. There is no convincing evidence that teenage boys do any less well when the custodial parent is mom rather than dad.

> Feeling inadequate is an occupational hazard of motherhood.

The most important issue for John is not where he lives but what kind of connection he has to both of his parents. It's an unusual teenager who doesn't test a parent's rules, and your commitment to hanging in with your son sends him an important message. Remember that all mothers—and fathers, for that matter—feel ineffectual at times. Resist the temptation to fire yourself!

Why Do Adopted Children Search?

Dear Harriet:

I read an article stating that children who are dissatisfied in their adopted homes are more apt to want to find their natural parents. Is this true?

Dear Reader:

Nothing could be further from the truth. The wish to gain clarity about one's roots and connect with one's biological parents is a normal and healthy part of answering the "Who am I?" question. The process, as complex and wrenching as it might be, is ultimately healing and strengthening.

Many adoptees feel constrained from learning about their biological parents and relatives. They experience their curiosity as disloyal or hurtful to their adoptive parents. We should

> Connecting with one's biological parents is ultimately strengthening.

applaud those parents who can comfortably and openly share information and give their children their blessings to explore their origins.

Of course, only an adoptee (or birth parent) can decide if and when the time is right to begin to search. But the need to know is normal and healthy. And there is an impressive body of research indicating that adoptees fare better when their origins are not shrouded in secrecy and silence, and when they can actively replace the void of the unknown with faces and facts.

Is It Really All My Fault?

Dear Harriet:

My nineteen-year-old daughter, Amy, has been in therapy for depression. When I visited her last summer, she took me with her to a therapy session and accused me of causing her problems. She even implied that I ruined her life. Her therapist said very little but appeared to agree. I feel both angry and guilty, and we're not speaking. Who should apologize first? Please help!

Dear Reader:

Almost all daughters will feel angry with their mothers at some point, because no mother can live up to the impossible expectations that accompany this role. Even therapists may hold mothers responsible for all family problems.

Sadly, mother-blaming is in our bones. But mothers do *not* single-handedly ruin their children or cause them to be sick. When things go wrong in a family, it's due to unresolved issues and complex family patterns that have existed over generations.

As a daughter gets older, and perhaps becomes a mother herself, this blaming stance is often softened and replaced by a more realistic and empathetic perspective. Keep in mind that most daughters blast their mothers somewhere along the way, if they are confident that their mothers are sturdy enough to take it. Most relationships survive these outbursts, and some are even strengthened by them.

It's understandable for you to feel both angry and guilty and for you to want your daughter to apologize. If you choose, you can wait for an apology from Amy, which may never come. Or you can take the initiative to reconnect with her in a calm and nondefensive fashion. Once she feels her anger has registered with you, she may begin to respond differently.

Deintensifying the situation requires that you stop doing all the things you do naturally when you are anxious or under attack. These include defending yourself, criticiz-

> Most daughters blast their mothers
> somewhere along the way, if they think
> their mothers are sturdy enough to take it.

ing Amy, trying to convince her of "the truth," or cutting her off entirely. Any or all of the above will only escalate the problem.

Before you contact Amy again, I suggest that you reflect on the history of mother-daughter relationships in your family. How is your relationship with Amy similar to and different from your relationship with your own mother? What do you know about your mother's relationship with *her* mother? Has there been a pattern of entrenched fighting or distance between parents and children in previous generations? Is one of your parents the "bad guy" in your eyes? Keep in mind that the problems you and Amy are experiencing are a legacy of your family and our culture, which goes back to a time long before either of you was born.

The best time to get in touch with Amy is when you feel calmer. You may want to drop her a note instead of calling her. Letters give both parties the time and space to think—rather than to react in the old, patterned ways. Here is an example of the kind of communication that could help ease tension:

Dear Amy,

It's been difficult for me to get back in touch since my visit. I've been trying to think about the things you said as objectively as possible. It's hard, because I get defensive when I feel criticized. But I'll keep trying. I really appreciate your wish to share your feelings with me, because I want to have the kind of relationship in which we can talk openly about important things. I know I wasn't able to listen very well during the therapy session, but it's a start.

Since my visit, I've been thinking more about my relationship with my mother. I was never able to tell her when I was angry with her, and I never really stood up to her. (Maybe that is why I get so nervous about conflict between you and me.) This made things easier at times, but it also made for a pretty distant and superficial relationship.

I also know that my mother fought all the time with her own mother. From the stories Mom tells, they were always at war. So, she and I reacted to that bit of history by doing the opposite and never letting a difference arise between us.

As I think about these patterns between the mothers and daughters in our family. I realize how much I hope that you and I can have a different kind of relationship. I know that won't be easy, but I love you and I want to work on it.

Love, Mom

Changing your relationship with Amy will be an ongoing challenge. She may continue to blame you, but what's important is how you handle your *own* steps in this dance.

No one conversation is pivotal. You *can* work on your relationship so that it gets better rather than worse over time.

A Bereaved Child

Dear Harriet:

My husband was killed in an automobile accident about a year ago. Since that time, my eight-year-old son, Willy, has been acting up. He makes huge messes in the apartment, demands that I buy him whatever he wants, and screams when I don't go along with his demands. Meanwhile, I'm finding I can't say no to a boy who has lost his father. My best friend says I'm too soft with him, but I feel such pity for my son and I desperately want to make up for his loss. Is it wrong to indulge him? Should I take him to a therapist?

Dear Reader:

It is understandable that you want to do everything possible to help your son at this difficult time. But most of all, Willy needs reassurance that you are competent to keep the family going and that you are in charge. He also needs you to encourage *his* competence, by establishing clear rules, expectations, and consequences for misbehavior.

Of course, Willy needs your love, comfort, and understanding, as well. But compassion is not the same as pity. Nor do children flourish in an "anything goes" atmosphere. Explain to Willy that it's normal for him to feel angry and upset about his dad's death and that it's OK for him to talk about it. But it's not OK for him to misbehave or treat others rudely. Let him know that you expect more from him.

Willy will test you many times to see if you *really* mean it. Ultimately, however, he will be strengthened and reas-

sured by your firmness, particularly if you can set limits
and enforce consequences calmly, without anger, intensity,
or blame. Of course, that's the ideal, not the reality of how
most families function in
the anxious aftermath of an
important loss.

> Your son needs
> reassurance that
> you can establish
> clear rules, expectations,
> and consequences
> for misbehavior.

Instead of putting Willy
into therapy, first seek a
consultation from a competent family therapist who is
experienced with grieving
families. Choose someone
who can offer you support
and practical guidance in dealing with Willy at this difficult
time. Willy can be included in sessions, but ultimately you
can help him most by seeking help for yourself through
therapy. Adults have far greater resources than children to
use therapy to solve problems, create more functional relationships, and alter the emotional climate of family life.

I'm sure you know that you can't make up for Willy's
loss, as much as you would like to. Both of you need time
to grieve and to get back in touch with the strengths you
have as a family. Be sure to stay connected to friends and
family members, including your deceased husband's relatives. When children lose a parent, they may also lose their
connections to that parent's family—to aunts, uncles, and
cousins.

Most important, take care of yourself. If you need to
indulge someone, start here. The loss of a spouse is a devastating experience. It is important for you to have help
and support for yourself during this difficult time.

I Can't Stop Worrying About My Daughter

Dear Harriet:

Our only child, Laurie, has left home to attend an out-of-state college. She is very happy. The problem is that I worry constantly about her safety, particularly because she is living in a big city. My husband says there is nothing to worry about and that my constant anxiety is driving him crazy. Is it normal to worry?

Dear Reader:

Sure, it's normal for a mother to worry about her daughter's safety. The world *is* unsafe, particularly for women. It's also normal for parents to have a hard time when their child (in this case, your first and last) leaves for college. It's an anxious time in the life cycle of any family.

Often, however, we put all our "worry energy" into one basket and fail to identify other sources of stress. When a child leaves home, all family members are called upon to make major emotional adjustments and to renegotiate their relationships. Try to place your worry within a broader context.

For example, how does Laurie's departure affect your marriage? Do you think that you and your husband will become closer or more distant over the next few years? Also, do you have a way to feel close to Laurie other than by worrying about her?

Suppose you could magically be assured that no harm would befall Laurie during her college years. Where would all your worry energy go? What plans do you have for *your* future, now that Laurie's gone? Do you have particular interests that you would like to develop? What might keep you from making and following your own life plan?

> When a child leaves home, all family members are called upon to renegotiate their relationships.

Learn more about the issue of leaving home in your own family of origin. What were you doing when you were Laurie's age, and how calm or anxious was your family at that time? Talk to other family members about what leaving home was like and how parents reacted when kids got launched. As our children move through the life cycle, our reactions are filtered through our own family history. You'll feel calmer if you can put your worry into a broader multigenerational perspective.

As an experiment, try not to express worry to your husband for several weeks and see what happens. If you begin to worry less, he may worry more. It's good to try to equalize the burden of parental worry—or at least to rotate it! And congratulations to both of you for having raised an independent daughter.

8
≋

The World
We Love In

Introduction

My first reaction to the women's liberation movement in the late sixties was one of disinterest. After all, what did it have to do with me? I had faced no discrimination in pursuing my degree in clinical psychology and I felt glad to be a woman.

The love that my husband and I shared was based on equality and mutual respect. Our relationship had never been a hierarchical one involving any static division of labor. I enjoyed my "feminine" prerogatives of being able to express tears, vulnerability, and silliness. And if I wasn't complaining, I didn't see why anyone else should be.

I also looked somewhat suspiciously upon the growing expressions of female anger and discontent. If women were feeling like glorified scullery maids, why didn't they get out of the kitchen? If they wanted to be treated like mature women, why did they refer to themselves as girls? Wasn't raising children a more creative and challenging task than the work most men did? And were not men equally oppressed by our rigid notions of masculinity?

Mainly, I felt sorry for the guys. I could think of no fate worse than being drafted, or, almost as bad, having to show up for work every day in the dull uniform of a suit and tie. As a psychologist, and a "liberated" one at that, I could not help but see the anger of the women's movement as a rationalization of neurotic internal conflicts. If women didn't like their place in life, why didn't they do something about it.

And yet I was also aware that women had hardly any choices at all. So from the beginning, I felt uncomfortable and dishonest in the face of my condescension to feminist protests. Although partially blinded by my arrogance at having "made it" in a man's world, I eventually had to face the fact that my criticism of feminism stemmed from my own resistance to looking squarely at my relationships with men, with women, and with myself.

Also, I just didn't *get* feminism. Before my own consciousness-raising, I didn't question the predominant myths of the day, or see beyond the male-defined reality I had accepted as a given. It was especially difficult to confront the fact that I, too, had lied to myself about my experience, fearing disapproval. I didn't want to be labeled one of those "angry women." I didn't want to be seen as a troublemaker. And I didn't want the burden of seeing discrimination where others pretended it didn't exist or didn't matter.

Perhaps my own initial defensiveness in response to the women's movement helps me to appreciate better the resistance of others. We all have anxiety about facing the fact that sexism is as complicated, as evil, and as deeply rooted as racism. Changing the way we live and relate to each other will always be a scary business. And because patriarchy is the only reality that we know, it's hard even to begin to imagine another way.

Also, there's something about our personal problems

that feels, well, *personal*. When we are reeling from a divorce, depression, or low self-esteem, we view the problem as our individual responsibility to be solved through our own initiative and effort. It's hard to see social and political inequalities as equally important in our lives. But they do count, and immeasurably so.

Although the connections are not always obvious, personal change is inseparable from social and political change. Intimate relationships cannot flourish in conditions of injustice and inequality. Not that it's easy to work for social justice, to speak out on our own behalf, or to make room to include others. As a recent college graduate candidly put it, "Diversity is exhausting, everyone feels offended, and all those different voices clamoring to be heard give me a headache."

The thing about consciousness-raising is that you can't go back to being a sleepwalker. Once you start noticing what groups of people are *included* and *valued* and *paid*—and what groups of people are not—there's no turning back. Even in these hard times, I'm glad to be around now, when women have arisen from a collective slumber to create passionate new visions of work, friendship, and community.

Girls, Ladies, or Women?
Does It Matter?

Dear Harriet:

Of all the politically correct language we are exhorted to use these days, I must protest the fuss surrounding the word *woman*. Personally, I prefer to be called a *lady* or a *girl*. Women must fight for equality, but we must choose our battles, and this one just doesn't matter.

Dear Reader:

Are you sure? Ponder the following headlines:

WOMEN MARCH FOR PEACE
LADIES MARCH FOR PEACE
GIRLS MARCH FOR PEACE

Do different images come to mind? Probably so. Only the word *woman* connotes status, authority, and seriousness of purpose. We don't think of a girl running for Congress or winning the Nobel Prize. We don't say, "How nice that President Clinton invited an African-American girl, Maya Angelou, to read a poem at his inauguration."

The word *lady* is reassuringly polite. It functions as a euphemism, removing the sexual, aggressive, and reproductive implication inherent in the word *woman*. Complete the following sentences, and you will see that the designations *woman* and *lady* are hardly synonymous:

- She feared that after her hysterectomy, she might not feel like a real _____.

- Jane is sweet, soft-spoken, and modest. She is truly a _____.

- When Sue began to menstruate, she knew she was on the road to becoming a _____.

- She felt passionate with him, like a wild _____.

When I'm being playful among close friends, I often use the term *girl*, but I bristle when I hear the word applied to me in other settings. Words are powerful and our choice of language both reflects and shapes attitudes. A *colored boy* is not the same as a *black man*. We separate the *men* from the *boys*. There is a difference between a *boy*, a *gentleman*, and a *man*. Let's not pretend that language doesn't make a difference.

> We don't think of a girl running for Congress or winning the Nobel Prize.

As you sit in a waiting room or stand in a checkout line, pay careful attention to the widespread avoidance of the word *woman*. The preferred use of the terms *girl, lady,* or *gal* often reflects an unconscious wish to define women in narrow, nonthreatening, or diminutive terms.

PC does not stand just for political correctness. As feminist Robin Morgan reminds us, it also stands for plain courtesy. If you want to be called a *girl* or *lady*, let people know. Your wishes should be respected. But please also understand that many of us do not share your preference.

Is Hope Possible in This Violent World?

Dear Harriet:

As I watch television and read the newspaper I increasingly lose faith in humanity and my hope for the future. In a world of endless war and violence how can I avoid feeling hopeless? How do you find a way to maintain any hope in such troubled times?

Dear Reader:

You might change what you read and watch, or at least enlarge it. The mainstream media focus relentlessly on violence and other calamities. Equal time and space are not given to the often remarkable and inspiring behavior of human beings everywhere, which is less frequently considered "hard news."

I maintain hope because I believe it's a moral imperative. As long as we *feel* hope, there *is* hope. But I do not naively or sentimentally assume that peace and justice will miraculously burst forth in our midst. The business of peace takes both faith and work. And, as Mahatma Gandhi said, "Peace between countries must rest on the solid foundation of love between individuals." So I feel most hopeful when I move toward others with a loving heart.

Whether we are speaking of warring couples or nations, it is an extraordinary challenge to move from blaming people toward understanding patterns and our own part in them. When, in my own work, I see individuals and families meet this challenge in the most difficult of circumstances, it reminds me of the possibilities of change—and keeps me humble by knowing how difficult it is.

Avoiding the F Word

Dear Harriet:

My friends and I have been fighting for women's rights for two decades. Ironically, our daughters, many of whom are college age, don't want to call themselves feminists. They seem to take the strides we have made for granted. Why do many young women avoid the word *feminist*? Do they really think the struggle is over? Also, could you define the word *feminist*?

Dear Reader:

If young women avoid the F word, it's not because their elders have succeeded in creating a world that includes and values women. We haven't. Anyone who takes the equality of women for granted is sleepwalking or, more accurately, in a coma.

Feminism continues to change and challenge all of our lives, whether or not we agree with what a particular feminist says. The feminist movement, like the civil rights movement, is a profoundly transforming, enlivening, and empowering social revolution. But because we have been *so* successful, the backlash against us has been virulent: violence against women has increased; women comprise a growing majority of our nation's poor; and our constitutional right to choose whether or not to reproduce is constantly threatened.

In the face of such a backlash one might expect all women to rush back to the broom closet, which has not happened. But it's hardly surprising that some young women hesitate to call themselves feminists, even when they support feminist aims. It's never been easy for women to take up our own cause (in contrast to fighting on behalf of others) because if we do so, we are still likely to be stereotyped. We may be referred to as one of those "angry women" or even accused of hating men. We may be labeled

> Anyone who takes the equality of women for granted is in a coma.

unloving or unfeminine—even strident, male-bashing, or castrating. Being on the receiving end of such pejorative labels is painful and can serve to silence us.

But not to worry. Feminism (or as many African-Americans prefer, *womanism*) is alive and well. Feminism continues to transform not only the world around us but also the hearts, minds, and souls of women and men. Like the human rights movement, the women's movement is powerful and broad-based. It will not go away, no matter how many mainstream writers announce the postfeminist era or report that feminism is dead. Women's voices can no longer be silenced or forgotten. Nor can we be erased from history and the future.

What is a feminist? As the writer Rebecca West said in 1913, "I myself have never been able to find out precisely what feminism is: I only know that people call me a feminist whenever I express sentiments that differentiate me from a doormat."

One of my favorite definitions comes from a poem that Alice Duer Miller wrote in 1915:

"Mother, what is a Feminist?"
"A Feminist, my daughter,
Is any woman now who cares
To think about her own affairs
As men don't think she oughter."

Color Does Matter

Dear Harriet:

I'm the only African-American woman in a study group that meets monthly. We are reading several books about mothers and daughters that are by white writers. When I mentioned this fact, I was told that color doesn't matter, that we're all more alike than different under the skin. So why do I feel so upset?

Dear Reader:

You're probably upset because the group's response is racist, although that may not be anyone's intention. Ask your group to change their reading list to reflect the rich diversity of the real world or, at the very least, the composition of its own members. There are many stories and poems about African-American mothers and daughters, including

> Being the only minority voice in an otherwise white group is not an optimal situation for learning.

writings by such notable women as Maya Angelou, Alice Walker, bell hooks, June Jordan, Sonia Sanchez, and others.

Being the only minority voice in an otherwise white group is not an optimal situation for learning. Perhaps you can invite more women of color into your group or join (or start) a different reading group that is more culturally diverse. In any case, don't remain in a group that mistakenly accepts the experience of the dominant culture as the experience of all humankind and that refuses to examine this undemocratic practice.

All the members of your current group will benefit from diversifying both the reading list and the membership. We can't even understand and appreciate *ourselves* when we narrow our attention to "our own kind."

Closets Are for Clothes

Dear Harriet:

I have nothing against homosexuals and I deplore prejudice of any kind. But I fail to see the importance of "coming out" for gays and lesbians. My husband and I do not discuss our sex life or sexual orientation in public, so why should homosexuals? What ever happened to privacy and discretion?

Dear Reader:

When certain folks hear the word *homosexual* the sexual part of the word flashes in their mind like a neon sign. But life for all of us extends far beyond what we do in the privacy of our bedrooms.

To be gay and in the closet is to watch oneself constantly. One doesn't say, "My partner and I are off to Florida!" One doesn't pull out a photo of one's soul mate to share with a co-worker. One doesn't step off the plane and freely embrace one's lover or hold hands by the baggage claim. One doesn't tell friends about a new volunteer job at the gay counseling center. Any of these ways of holding back, of not speaking, of not acting, may seem trivial. But over time, silence and secrecy erode dignity, spontaneity, self-regard, and joy. The right to live and love openly—and to be who we are—are the most precious rights we have.

Prejudice has many faces, and enforced invisibility is no less damaging than outright hate, which at least acknowledges that one does, indeed, exist. A lesbian friend reminds me that she feels erased almost daily from the cat-

egories of "humans" and "women." She attends panels and
workshops on "Love in the Nineties," or "Adjusting to
Mastectomy," or "Mothers and Daughters." Not only do the
programs omit issues specific to lesbians, but the experts
talk as if homosexuals don't
exist at all. Heterosexuals
take themselves to be "it," or
"what counts," and deny the
reality that homosexuals are
everywhere.

> I wouldn't want
> someone to say of
> my Jewishness:
> "It's unfortunate, but
> she was born that way."

Lesbians and gays do
not want tolerance, but
rather, visibility, celebration,
and inclusion. No self-respecting group of people could
ask for less. I'm sure it's no different from the way I feel
about my Jewishness. I wouldn't want folks to say, "It's
unfortunate, but, after all, she was born that way"—or
(about my son's bar mitzvah), "Well, I think it's fine that
the Lerners are Jewish, but must they *flaunt* it?" I wouldn't
want to be told that in the name of privacy and discretion,
I should lie, conceal, and pretend each day to be what I'm
not.

An old popular song tells us, "Everybody loves a
lover." Maybe one day those words will truly include us all,
and no one will feel they have to hide the honest affections
of the heart.

Are Women Too Dependent?

Dear Harriet:

I'm a third-year college student, and my philosophy professor said in class that he prefers the company of men because women are too dependent. Are women really more dependent than men? His comment made me angry, but maybe I'm overreacting.

Dear Reader:

Dependency, we are told, is a bad characteristic that women presumably possess more of than men. This is a questionable assumption at best, since emotional dependency is a universal aspect of human experience. Men do seem better at hiding their dependency, though—even from themselves—primarily because the women in their lives are often so good at predicting and attending to their needs.

Contrary to your professor, I believe that women are not dependent enough. Women tend to be far more skilled at attending to the dependency needs of others than in identifying and assertively claiming our own needs. Moreover, it is not our emotional dependency on men but our *economic* dependency, especially in marriage, that puts us in a position of profound vulnerability.

Other women in your class probably shared your reaction to your professor's statement. But even if you're alone with your anger, your response to his comment doesn't mean you're oversensitive, just awake.

Women Who Read Too Much

Dear Harriet:

My problems with relationships and low self-esteem have led me to read lots of psychological self-help books for women. I'm filled with hope when I start them, but then I lose my motivation and feel bad about myself. I find that experts give different and even contradictory advice. What do you think of self-help books? How does a reader know what to believe? How can I choose the books that are best for me?

Dear Reader:

We can't be cautious enough in approaching the whole advice-giving industry. Self-help books for women are part of a multibillion-dollar business, sensitively attuned to our insecurities and our purses. There are countless books on the market that women learn to eat up like popcorn in our endless and impossible pursuit of perfection.

Many of these books simplify human experience with platitudes, inspirational messages, recipes for success, and explain-everything guides to personal empowerment, self-esteem, and relational bliss. As a journalist once said, self-help books explain life the way Cliff Notes explain Tolstoy. Also, far more remains unknown than known about emotional struggles, and there are countless ways to name, frame, or tackle a particular problem.

Women have always been the primary consumers of self-help books. No wonder, given our culture's relentless focus on improving and perfecting women. If only women would attract men more or want them less, do better at balancing work and family, embrace the wounded child or the goddess within, twelve-step our way out of trouble, or somehow solve our own personal problems—then men and their institutions would not have to change.

> No book will bring you ecstatic sex,
> high self-esteem, or an escape from the range
> of painful emotions that make us human.

But it's also a great strength of women to value relationships, and our selves, and to seek help. Acquiring skills to enhance our self-regard, as well as our connectedness with friends, lovers, kin, and the universe, is undeniably a good idea. So, in keeping with my own advice-giving leanings, here's a list of six dos and don'ts that may help you confront the self-help section of your bookstore.

1. *Don't believe authors who make large and silly promises.* A self-help book won't bring you ecstatic sex, high self-esteem, or an escape from the range of painful emotions that make us human. Substantive change occurs slowly over time, with many frustrations and derailments. The good news is that sometimes a small change will make a big difference in your life.

2. *Do take a good tip wherever you find it.* In one self-help book a woman shares her strategic response to obscene phone calls. She asks the offender, "Would you please repeat that—I'm a little hard of hearing." When he does, she says, "I'm sorry, I still don't get it—would you please speak up?" If the offender still doesn't hang up on her, she asks him to repeat himself until he does. This worked for me and in itself gave me enough satisfaction to justify the price of the book.

3. *Don't buy books that promote guilt.* Women feel guilty enough and should not pay money to be made to feel more guilty.

4. *Do take expert advice as just one opinion.* Maintain a healthy skepticism toward authors who presume to have a corner on the truth. Nothing is normal, right, or true for all women. At best, experts have a partial perspective, which may or may not be useful to you. Run with good advice and ignore the rest.

5. *Don't buy books that promote a narrow, blaming attitude toward family members.* Families are not fair, and we do not choose the family we are born into. As adults, we nonetheless are accountable for how we navigate our part within these relationships. A good self-help book can provide creative options for changing your part in family patterns without promoting self-blame and without disqualifying legitimate anger and hurt. Family problems are generations in the making.

6. *Do try to find books that engage your heart and mind.* Trust your evaluations and gut reactions, including negative ones. If you fail to change, why not blame the book, rather than yourself?

When the student is ready, the teacher arrives—and sometimes in the form of a great book. Many authors have valuable expertise on women's lives. Also, a self-help book is far less expensive and time-consuming than either psychotherapy or psychoanalysis. And much easier to get out of when it's just not helping.

Are Women 50 Percent to Blame for Sexism?

Dear Harriet:

I know that sexism exists. But women make up more than half of this country's population and apparently we accept patriarchy. If we're not insisting on equality, and asserting our needs, aren't women themselves half the problem?

Dear Reader:

Many women are complicitous with sexist solutions, but no—we're not half the problem. Patriarchy won't fall just because women assert that it should. It's difficult to really *see* patriarchy, much less protest it, because it's the only reality we know.

As the physicist Fritjof Capra wrote more than a decade ago: "The power of patriarchy has been extremely difficult to understand because it is all pervasive. It has influenced our most basic ideas about human nature and about our relation to the universe. . . . It is the one system which, until recently, had never in recorded history been openly challenged, and whose doctrines were so universally accepted that they seemed to be laws of nature."

History teaches us that no dominant group has ever relinquished power voluntarily. And no subordinate group has ever protested its own subordination without taking risks and incurring punishment. It took the better part of a century before women were granted the right to vote—and then only after years of mass organizing and struggle that included picketing, demonstrations, jailings, and hunger strikes—after more "ladylike" tactics failed. During this time, a number of society's prominent experts argued that to grant women equality in this sphere would threaten the very fabric of American society and corrupt women's God-given nature.

> Women are responsible for ending men's monopoly on power, for the simple reason that no one else will do it for us.

Institutionalized resistance of this order and magnitude remains alive and well today, making it difficult for women—individually and collectively—to protest or even to see the full range of inequalities that make protest necessary.

Still, we should take your question to heart, as a challenge of the highest order. Whether women are 2 percent or 92 percent to blame for the inequality, we are more than 50 percent of the population and we can cast seven million more votes than men. And we are responsible for ending men's monopoly on power, for the simple reason that no one else will do it for us.

My Husband Has a Persecution Complex

Dear Harriet:

I am a white woman of German descent, married for two years to an African-American man, Bill. It took great effort to convince Bill to go to marital therapy with me, and now he wants to quit. He sees all his problems in terms of skin color, so he's frustrated with our white therapist, who won't let him hide behind racism. How can I help Bill to get off his soap box, get past his anger and persecution complex, and stay in therapy? As the therapist and I constantly point out, many white people—myself included—deal with as much (or more) unfairness in the world as Bill does.

Dear Reader:

All humans experience unfairness, but unfairness is not the same as racism. There are countless advantages that white skin confers, including the privilege of not thinking about skin color. You probably don't give your whiteness a thought when you go to rent an apartment, apply for a job, hail a taxi at night, or get pulled over by a policeman for speeding. If you stay at an expensive hotel, you need not worry about being stereotyped as a housekeeper.

> Your husband is wise to question any therapist who minimizes the profound, ongoing effects of racism.

Bill doesn't have this prerogative of forgetting about his skin color and the stereotypes that accompany it.

Dr. Peggy McIntosh has identified the many ways "white privilege" is a pervasive reality that remains invisible to those who have it. She writes, "I have come to see white privilege as an invisible package of unearned assets which I can count on cashing in each day, but about which I was 'meant' to remain oblivious. White privilege is like an invisible weightless knapsack of special provisions, assurances, tools, maps, guides, codebooks, passports, visas, clothes, compass, emergency gear, and blank checks." If we remain oblivious to white privilege, we can't get past racism. Whites live in a different world altogether from the one that Bill lives in.

As for psychotherapy, most therapists, being human, are deeply uncomfortable with the subject of racism. So Bill is wise to question any therapist who minimizes the profound, ongoing effects of racism or who communicates a "Can't you get past this already!" attitude. Bill deserves a therapist who provides a safe place for him to express his anger and who validates the inseparability of his personal problems and his cultural heritage as an African-American male. He also deserves a therapist with whom he feels "at home." Only after these conditions are met, can Bill begin to examine whether his focus on racism is obscuring other issues from his view.

Finally, any therapy will stay stuck if the therapist is in an alliance with one spouse, trying to convince the other of "the truth." So if the marriage is your priority, ask Bill if he'd consider marital therapy with a new therapist, if he's uncomfortable with the process you're currently in.

Tired of the Victim Mentality

Dear Harriet:

I agree with feminist goals, but not with feminist anger or blame. If women view themselves as victims of men, or of society, we will be powerless to change anything. Blaming only keeps people stuck, so why do it? I for one am tired of hearing words like *oppression* and *victimization* applied to women. I am not a passive victim! And men are not to blame!

Dear Reader:

If you don't like the word *victim* or the images of women you associate with it, then don't use it. We should eliminate those words from our personal vocabularies that we find disempowering or dispiriting. We all need to embrace language that enhances our capacity to imagine and to act.

But don't be so quick to equate the word *victim* with powerlessness or passivity. Even the most angry feminists do not sit in a corner passively bemoaning their victimized status. To the contrary, a realistic appraisal of oneself or women as a group as victimized, oppressed, or subordinate is necessary if women are to speak out effectively and take action on our own behalf.

From the beginning of modern feminism, women who openly voiced anger were active agents of social change. They were busy writing women back into language, history, and politics, discovering women's roots in prior generations, and establishing countless programs and services central to women's lives. In fact, it's precisely

because anger is a vehicle for change that society discour-
ages women from voicing it.

Is blaming useful? *Blaming* is a word used glibly in ref-
erence to feminists. Like *nagging*, the word *blaming* is
fraught with negative connotations, and with some good
reason. When we overfocus on what the other party is
doing wrong, we underfocus on our part of the problem
and our options for acting differently. Blaming can lead
men and women to become increasingly polarized and can
mitigate against effective problem solving that considers
the needs of all.

> Men do not sit around in smoke-filled rooms
> with maps and pins figuring out
> how to oppress women.

But blaming can also be necessary and productive.
Members of subordinate groups naturally experience
strong anger when they are able to see beyond the dominant group's definition of reality to identify clearly their
own subordinate status. This anger reflects dignity and self-
regard and is an essential milestone in the process of liberation.

The familiar phrase "But men are not to blame!" is
true on one level. Men do not sit around in smoke-filled
rooms with maps and pins figuring out how to oppress
women. But the taboos against blaming men serve to
silence female anger and maintain the status quo. The
struggle of any subordinate group is weakened when its
members' anger and frustration are disqualified by the
argument that those in power are not to blame for anything or that the expression of anger itself denotes a lack
of clarity, judgment, or maturity. For women, it is most

often the failure to identify our subordinate status, combined with excessive fear of female anger, that leaves us powerless to effect change.

Labeling *all* men villains and *all* women victims is admittedly not a productive strategy for change. And we may have good reason to dislike the tactics of a particular feminist. But we should remember that feminist anger has created one of the most profound shifts in consciousness the world has seen, through one of the most humane and bloodless revolutions the world has ever known.

Whose Truth Counts?

Dear Harriet:

I'm confused about where I stand on the abortion issue. On some days I think I'm definitely pro-choice. On other days, I think about the unborn fetus and I feel the opposite. I've never been faced with an unwanted pregnancy, but I know it would be traumatic. I wonder if you would share your personal feelings on this issue and how you see the truth of the matter.

Dear Reader:

I obtained a safe and legal abortion when an unexpected pregnancy followed soon after the birth of my second son. Because I was treated with respect and care—and because I had just completed the family I planned for—the abortion was not traumatic. What is traumatic is the idea that I could be forced to carry and give birth to a child involuntarily—that my body, spirit, will, and the direction of my life would no longer be my own. To imagine myself pregnant, and without choice, is to send fear radiating to the very edges of my imagination.

These are my personal feelings—but what is the truth of the matter? The truth is that there is no truth on which we can all agree. And no wonder. When we arrive at our views on abortion, we draw on personal values and beliefs that emerge from our unique family histories and ethnic traditions. We are further influenced by our deepest unconscious wishes, longings, and fears about such large subjects as life and death, birth and loss, sacrifice and entitlement, women, reproduction, and motherhood. It's no surprise that people see the abortion issue differently.

We know how difficult it is to change another person. Nor are we ourselves readily converted. My own views on abortion are deeply held. Although I consider myself an open-minded person, the chances of my changing sides on the abortion issue are about as great as the chances of my dropping my Jewish religion when the next Jehovah's Witness knocks on my front door.

We can't eliminate our differences on the abortion issue, nor will those differences go away. We can, at best, learn to deal fairly and respectfully with opposing views rather than trying to force all people to examine a complex emotional issue through the same filter. I hope you will continue to listen to the different voices within yourself on the abortion question, rather than trying to silence or suppress any part of your complex response.

> Let's respect our differences rather than trying to force everyone to examine a complex emotional issue through the same filter.

So here's the bottom line—the ultimate challenge posed by the abortion controversy. Given our differences, who should be in charge of a reproductive decision for me or for you? Should a minister, rabbi, or physician have the final word? Should the decision be dictated by whichever group exerts the most powerful economic and political force of the day? Do we take a neighborhood vote?

I hope that instead we will rise to the challenge of respecting differences and individual choice. Such mutual respect requires us to develop humility—to recognize that it is our job to become the best expert on ourselves, not on our neighbors.

Finding the Right Therapist

Dear Harriet:

A close friend recommended a feminist therapist to help me overcome depression. But I don't want a therapist who wants to liberate me or impose her values. When my baby was born, I chose to put my career on hold and stay home, and I want a therapist who will respect my choices. Should I find a traditional therapist who will be neutral? How do feminist therapists work? How biased or competent are they?

Dear Reader:

The label *feminist therapist* tells us only that the therapist calls herself a feminist. It tells us nothing about the therapist's competence, education, experience, wisdom— or lack of these. Nor does it tell us anything about how the therapist actually conducts therapy.

Your concern about finding a female therapist who respects your choices is important. But feminist therapists don't impose their values on their clients, any more than nonfeminist therapists do. All therapists are products of their families and culture, and all therapists hold values and beliefs that they transmit, however unwittingly, to their clients.

In truth, their is *no* value-free therapy. The questions a therapist raises or does not raise, the interventions she makes or fails to think of, what she focuses on or ignores— all these reflect the therapist's worldview and assumptions about gender arrangements. Moreover, therapists, like people in general, are typically unaware of their own biases. You're unlikely to find a therapist who says, "Hi, I'm Doctor Smith and I will be conducting therapy from a patriarchal perspective."

I'd personally question the objectivity of any therapist who doesn't take feminism seriously and hasn't been changed by it. Gender, like race and class, is a primary determinant of an

> Don't start (or stay) in a therapy process that doesn't feel right for you.

individual's sense of power, possibility, and place in the world. A therapist who ignores or trivializes feminism is no more objective than a therapist who treats black clients as if racism doesn't exist or doesn't matter.

Interview any prospective therapist with care, and address your concerns and questions right up front. Trust your evaluation and gut reactions, including negative ones. Don't start (or stay) in a therapy process that doesn't feel right for you, no matter how highly the therapist is acclaimed or recommended by others.

Hurt by Racial Prejudice

Dear Harriet:

As a Puerto Rican single mother, I am often hurt by racial prejudice. My question is "Why?" My father says it's the natural condition of human beings to love each other but we are taught to hate. I disagree. It seems people naturally stick to their own kind and dislike people who are different. If prejudice is natural, why should we struggle or even care? We will never end discrimination.

Dear Reader:

I'm a psychologist, not an evolutionary biologist, so I view the nature-versus-nurture question through this lens.

Nothing is more natural than our human capacity to love. However, it also appears to be natural for humans to behave badly under certain conditions. When anxiety is high and resources appear scarce, some individuals and groups will always act at the expense of others. There is never a resting place in the struggle for personal dignity and political integrity.

Undeniably, our species has a poor track record for dealing with differences. We learn to hate or glorify differences, to exaggerate or ignore them. Either extreme gets us into trouble. It requires a rare degree of maturity for people under stress to respect differences, to view them objectively, and to maintain a capacity for problem solving that considers the needs of all.

Are we biologically programmed to diminish other humans in response to our own fear or unhappiness? Certainly not *all* humans are so programmed. Many people

> When anxiety is high and resources appear
> scarce, some individuals and groups will
> always act at the expense of others.

long passionately for justice and never compromise their
integrity and loving regard for others, no matter how terrible their personal circumstances.

More important, it doesn't matter whether a behavior
is natural or learned. Most human behaviors are insepara-
bly both. Whether a particular behavior is 9 percent or 90
percent natural tells us nothing about whether we should
accept it, cultivate it, or struggle against it. As Ogden Nash
succinctly put it, "Small pox is natural; vaccine ain't."

We cannot *not* affect our world. Either we act in ways
that enhance, include, and regard people, or we do the
opposite. I agree that we will never see an end to discrimination and prejudice. But if we don't stand up to racist
attitudes—and examine our own—then where do we
stand?

I'm Uncomfortable Excluding Men

Dear Harriet:

A neighbor gave me a subscription to a feminist newspaper for my birthday. I'm uncomfortable reading a feminist publication because it is separatist. Separatism is wrong today because women are well represented in the mainstream media, which report news objectively. Why do women feel the need for a biased newspaper that excludes men?

Dear Reader:

Comedienne Kate Clinton says, "When women go off together we call it separatism. When men go off together we call it Congress."

I share her sentiments. The same women who are worried and guilty about excluding men may fail to notice when women are included in only token numbers, or not included at all.

The mainstream media does not truly include women. And what women think and do is rarely considered "hard news." Susan B. Anthony addressed the need for feminist publications in 1893: "As long as newspapers and magazines are controlled by men . . . women's ideas and deepest convictions will never get before the public." Now, more than one hundred years later, her words are still relevant.

The feminist publication you are receiving may well have a biased perspective—but then, so do *Time, Newsweek,* and every major daily newspaper in the country. Editorial decisions about what merits inclusion and what is consid-

> What women think and do is rarely considered "hard news."

ered news reflect gender bias and a variety of other biases as well.

We're all biased; that is, we see the world through a filter that excludes more than it includes. So take the opportunity to read a wide variety of publications in order to move toward a more objective, inclusive, and enlarged perspective on what's new (and news) in the world.

Am I an Addict?

Dear Harriet:

Many of my friends are in twelve-step recovery groups for various addictions. A counselor friend of mine diagnosed me as having a "sex and relationship addiction" and wants me to join a twelve-step program to work on this. I don't like to call myself an addict, since I don't take drugs or alcohol. He says I'm in denial. I have mixed feelings about the recovery movement and would like your opinion.

Dear Reader:

I, too, have mixed feelings about the recovery movement, which, like most things, includes the good and the bad.

In the good category, recovery groups have helped countless women to take better care of themselves, both in and out of relationships. The recovery movement has provided women with a strong sense of community, support, and validation, and has paid respectful attention to lesbian relationships, usually rendered invisible by the self-help movement. The recovery movement has encouraged women to speak openly about how experiences such as alcoholism and sexual abuse have affected us, and has facilitated healing through a grassroots movement that has saved many lives. These are large achievements.

In the bad category, the recovery movement can lull women away from political activism and back into self-blaming and parent-blaming, back into diagnostic labels, negative self-definitions, and a narrow disease model of our problems and pain. Some women feel most comfortable moving forward in the name of recovery, perhaps because our society (never fond of "those angry women") is not threatened by sick women meeting together to get well.

Moreover, with everyone jumping on the recovery bandwagon, the term *addiction* has been globalized to include all the predictable, patterned behaviors that human beings use to lower anxiety. The recovery literature documents our addictions to sex, food, caretaking, relationships, romance, fantasies, work, crises, shopping, and laziness. When we use the term *addiction* in this vastly inclusive way, we erase and trivialize the anguish of individuals and families whose lives are devastated by actual physiological addictions.

If you think that a particular twelve-step recovery group may have something to offer you, by all means try it out and see. Many women say that the recovery movement saved their lives. But don't call yourself an addict— indeed, don't call yourself *anything* that feels diminishing, pathologizing, dispiriting, or just plain "off."

> The term *addiction* has been globalized to include almost everything.

Happy Mother's Day

Dear Harriet:

Maybe I'm jaded, but I don't want my family to celebrate one more Mother's Day. I love my kids but I'm tired of flowers and cards. It just feels like a lot of commercial hype. Given the lack of political clout women have in the world, and how little real respect mothers are given for the work they do, who needs all this flowery sentimentality? Am I the only one who resents Mother's Day?

Dear Reader:

I'm sure many folks share your feelings. But here's the true meaning of Mother's Day, which is the greatest story never (or rarely) told. I learned this bit of lost history from educator Joan Lester, in her book *The Future of White Men and Other Diversity Dilemmas.*

> The true meaning of Mother's Day is the
> greatest story never told.

Mother's Day originated in 1870 as an appeal to women to leave the home for an "earnest day of counsel" in which women would meet together to influence international issues of the day. The first Mother's Day proclamation began with the words, "Arise, then, women of this day!" It was a call to public action.

The Mother's Day proclamation urged women to take public policy into their own hands. It also asked women to stop supporting men who weren't dedicated to seeking peaceful settlements of international conflict. "Our husbands shall not come to us, reeking with carnage, for caresses and applause," the proclamation continued.

Mother's Day was born out of the suffragist movement of the 1850s and 1860s when women joined together to fight slavery and seek the vote. How fascinating that the bold history of Mother's Day has become transformed into a sanctification of women's domestic role.

I agree with Lester's suggestion that we celebrate Mother's Day by remembering its origins—and that we honor our mothers and foremothers best by remembering that a woman's sphere is rightly regarded as the world. No false sentimentality here.

About the Author

Dr. Harriet Lerner is a clinical psychologist and psychotherapist at the Menninger Clinic in Topeka, Kansas. She is an internationally renowned expert on the psychology of women, and a distinguished lecturer, consultant, and workshop leader.

Born in Brooklyn, New York, Dr. Lerner did her undergraduate work at the University of Wisconsin in Madison and pursued independent research in Delhi, India. She received her M.A. in Educational Psychology from Teacher's College of Columbia University and her Ph.D. in Clinical Psychology from the City University of New York.

Dr. Lerner writes a monthly advice column in *New Woman* magazine called "Harriet Lerner's Good Advice." She is the author of a bestselling trilogy, *The Dance of Anger, The Dance of Intimacy,* and *The Dance of Deception,* which has sold more than two million copies and been translated into thirty foreign editions.

Her book *Women in Therapy* is considered a classic in the field. She is also the coauthor of several children's books with her sister, Susan Goldhor.

Dr. Lerner lives in Topeka, Kansas, with her husband, Steve. They have two sons, Matt and Ben.